# MODERN LANGUAGE TESTING
## A HANDBOOK

# MODERN LANGUAGE TESTING
## A HANDBOOK

**REBECCA M. VALETTE**
*Boston College*

**HARCOURT, BRACE & WORLD, INC.**
*New York / Chicago / San Francisco / Atlanta*

*dedicated to the memory of*

**George A. C. Scherer**

*teacher and friend*

# FOREWORD

For a decade and a half the study of modern foreign languages in American schools and colleges has been marked by new objectives, new instructional materials, and new teaching methods. These new goals and techniques have resulted in great improvement in most areas of language instruction. The revolution cannot, however, be considered complete when one of the major elements of foreign-language teaching—measurement—still shows weaknesses that threaten to invalidate the progress made in other areas. Too many foreign-language methods courses, too many courses of study and curriculum guides, and too many research projects are still characterized by poor measurement instruments and procedures. It is the classroom teacher, especially the one who is attempting to reach the new objectives via the new techniques, who feels perhaps the greatest need for guidance in this important but often neglected phase of the new key in language instruction.

Professor Valette has produced a handbook that goes far toward filling this need. The classroom teacher will want to read and study it and refer to it repeatedly as new situations arise. Teachers of beginning courses will be especially pleased with the suggestions for testing achievement in listening and speaking. The standard answer sheet, the scale for rating intonation and fluency, and the sound discrimination tests will find a welcome audience.

Before turning to the specific aids provided in Part Two (Chapters 5–9), the teacher should be sure to read and reread Part One. He will find—not immediately, but after some use of the handbook—that Chapter 4 contains the most useful advice for long-range improvement in his testing practices.

The more time the teacher spends in becoming acquainted with this handbook, the greater will be the improvement in his testing and instruction. The teacher will find Professor Valette's work a practical primer that will lead him to explore additional means for improving his measurement procedures.

F. ANDRÉ PAQUETTE

*Assistant Secretary for Foreign Languages*
*Modern Language Association of America*

# PREFACE

In the past twenty years a number of new methods of teaching language have appeared. These methods have been based largely on the results of research in learning theory and linguistics; their acceptance has been helped by an increased use of electronic equipment and by the financial and intellectual backing of the federal government, the Modern Language Association, and far-sighted members of the profession. The foreign-language teacher now has available to him an abundance of texts and other instructional materials that suggest the sequential development of the four fundamental skills of listening, speaking, reading, and writing.

It is clear that these new methods of teaching require new methods of evaluation. This handbook introduces the teacher to a diversity of testing techniques based on modern measurement theory; the book's emphasis, however, is on the classroom situation, theory being introduced only when it has a direct application for the teacher. Many examples have been given to help the teacher prepare tests that will effectively evaluate proficiency in the four fundamental skills. A special section also discusses literature tests.

The terminology of traditional grammar has been used in most instances instead of the more precise vocabulary of the linguists so that even teachers without formal training in modern linguistics will find the handbook convenient and useful. With a better understanding of measurement through the development and interpretation of the types of objective classroom tests suggested, the teacher should also be better able to evaluate commercial tests in relation to the goals he has set for his class.

In the preparation of this book I have incurred obligations to many people. I should like to thank Lewis Mayhew, Clifford Stewart, and Robert Morgenroth, who initiated me into the field of foreign-language testing; Pierre Delattre and A. P. van Teslaar, who introduced me to experimental phonetics and the evaluation of speech production; and John B. Carroll for his recommendations on achievement tests. The late George A. C. Scherer was particularly helpful with advice and inspiration. Nelson Brooks and Gerhard Loose have made suggestions on content and style throughout the entire manuscript. Ernest Siciliano checked the Italian and Spanish examples. André Paquette, Harold Bligh, and Neale Austin helped in the preparation of the Bibliography and the Appendix. To all these as well as to my husband, Jean-Paul Valette, for his careful reading of the manuscript and for his patience and encouragement, I wish to express my sincere gratitude.

Rebecca M. Valette

*Chestnut Hill, Massachusetts*

# CONTENTS

# INTRODUCTION
# HOW TO USE
# THIS
# HANDBOOK

To obtain maximum assistance from a handbook, the user must be familiar with its organization. Since this book is not intended to be used with one particular course of study or for one particular level of instruction, we have adopted the following format:

Part One presents the principles upon which tests should be constructed, a description of procedures, and an explanation of the terms that will be used in the remainder of the book.

Part Two contains practical suggestions for the construction of classroom tests. We realize that all textbooks or courses introduce vocabulary and the elements of grammar in slightly different sequences. The sounds of the new language are also presented in various ways, one of the most common being the learning of a dialogue. Rather than adopt the order of presentation of any one textbook or course, we have classified the types of tests and sample items according to the four language skills: listening, speaking, reading, and writing. This system was selected because a majority of today's language texts use audio-lingual methods and are directed to the development of student proficiency in these skills. Although the skills are obviously intermingled in the target language, and subsequently in its instruction, we feel that the teacher should be aware of which skill or combination of skills is being directly or indirectly tested. In the description of test items, considerable use has been made of contrastive structure studies. The types of items shown offer a generous sampling of the various methods at the teacher's disposal for assessing the progress of the students, but these suggestions are by no means exhaustive. The purpose of this book is to introduce the teacher to the wide possibilities of testing. Not only should the variety of tests help the teacher to construct more precise examinations, but it should enable him to offer his students livelier and more challenging tests.

A comprehensive index at the end of this handbook will allow the teacher to find easily the appropriate items to test the material being studied in a given course unit. Boldface page numbers indicate pages on which terms are defined.

# MODERN
# LANGUAGE
# TESTING
## A HANDBOOK

# PART ONE
# PRINCIPLES
# AND
# PROCEDURES

# CHAPTER ONE
# TESTING — ITS
# ROLE IN THE
# CLASSROOM

Since the end of World War II, language teachers in the United States have been broadening their aims and developing a curriculum designed to build up student proficiency in the skills of listening, speaking, reading, and writing. Standardized language tests have incorporated new evaluation techniques intended to provide a more precise measurement of student achievement. Yet it is important that the teacher himself know which aspects of a foreign language are measured by specific items and that he understand the role of testing in the classroom.

## 1.1 COURSE OBJECTIVES

Before determining a testing program for a specific course—indeed, before setting out to teach a course—the teacher should clearly envision his course objectives. By so doing he will be sure that his teaching will be rationally oriented and that his tests will indicate how close each student has come to attaining the objectives.

### 1.1.1 *Long-Range Objectives*

The long-range objectives play an essential role in defining the nature of the language program.

The most frequent overall objectives of a coordinated elementary-, junior-high-, and high-school language program are to enable the student to enjoy the literature written in the target language, to appreciate the culture of the target country, and especially to converse freely with its people. Students, in gaining proficiency in another language, learn to appreciate more deeply the vital role of all languages, including their native tongue, in human activity.[1]

### 1.1.2  *Short-Range Objectives*

Short-range objectives pertain to a specific course. The teacher or course coordinator decides how much of the phonology, the structure, and the vocabulary of the target language is to be mastered at each level of instruction. At the same time the decision must be made as to which skills are to be developed, in what order, and to what extent. For example, are certain structures and lexical items to be learned only passively (through reading, listening, or a combination)? Is the student to read only what he already can express fluently in speech? Should Ph.D. candidates in non-language fields concentrate only on the acquisition of the skill of reading? Time spent clarifying objectives is never wasted; on the contrary, clearly defined objectives are the requisite for effective teaching and efficient testing.

## 1.2  TYPES OF LANGUAGE TESTS

The distinction must first be made between the four types of language tests: prognostic, progress, achievement, and proficiency.[2] Each type of test is designed to measure certain qualities.

### 1.2.1  *The Prognostic Test*

The prognostic, or aptitude, test provides a statistical indication of a student's probable success in his study of a foreign language. While some students either score well on the prognostic test and do poorly in foreign-language class or obtain a low score on the prognostic test and yet perform well in class, prognostic test scores can be of assistance to guidance counselors. It should not be forgotten that personal motivation does play an important role.

---

[1] For a more extensive discussion of long-range objectives, see Nelson Brooks, *Language and Language Learning*, 2nd ed. (New York: Harcourt, Brace & World, 1964), chap. 8, and UNESCO, *The Teaching of Modern Languages* (Paris: UNESCO, 1955), chaps. 1–2.
[2] This distinction was first clearly made by Brooks, *op. cit.*, pp. 202–06.

**1.2.2**  *The Progress Test*

The progress test measures the extent to which a student has mastered
the material being taught in the classroom and the language laboratory. Although some textbook publishers have brought out progress tests to accompany their textbooks, most tests of this sort are prepared by the teacher
himself.

Since the classroom teacher in his daily work is primarily concerned with
progress tests, Part Two of this book will discuss their construction in detail.

**1.2.3**  *The Achievement Test*

Although the achievement test also measures the student's control of the
language, it is not based on the content of a particular course of instruction.
Such a test is generally prepared by an outside group of examiners and has
been carefully pretested and standardized; student raw scores may be compared to statewide or national norms. The achievement test is valid only
within the limits of its stated objectives.

**1.2.4**  *The Proficiency Test*

The proficiency test defines a student's level of achievement in reference to
a specific type of employment or instruction. The examiner wishes to ascertain not how much the student knows (as is the case with the achievement
test), but whether he has mastered specific skills and content deemed pre-
requisites for a particular job or course of study.

The placement test is the best-known of the proficiency tests. Such tests
are widely used at the college level, where large groups of incoming students
with different types of preparation must be assigned to various advanced
language classes. Large high schools with a rich language offering might
well investigate the possibility of developing a set of placement tests to
evaluate the proficiency of transfer students.

For maximum effectiveness, the placement test should be constructed by
the school or college itself. For each course the requisite level of preparation
should be determined, and the test should be designed specifically to measure
the knowledge and skills needed for success. If commercial tests are used,
the scores on these tests, or more precisely the scores on different parts of the
tests, should be interpreted in the light of the school's course requirements.
The MLA Proficiency Tests (see Appendix) have recently been developed
to ascertain the level of competence of language teachers and advanced
students.

## 1.3   PRINCIPLES OF CLASSROOM TESTING

The language teacher obviously desires to make optimum use of allotted time. Just as classroom work and laboratory practice should be carefully coordinated in order that both contribute to the attainment of a particular course objective, so should the testing program, modest though it may appear, be developed in accord with that objective.

### 1.3.1   *Defining the Classroom Objectives*

Students, particularly older ones, are quick to observe the types of tests given and to study accordingly. Thus, much as the teacher may emphasize oral fluency in the classroom, if all the tests are written tests the students will soon concentrate on perfecting the skills of reading and writing. If the teacher explains to the students that the course is intended to teach them how to manipulate the language with near-native fluency and then persists in giving tests composed of translations and declension tables, the students will continually refer to traditional grammatical terms and English equivalents.

Therefore, in a very real way the classroom tests define the short-range course objectives of the teacher. If beginning students are expected to develop primarily the skills of listening and speaking, then listening and speaking tests must be given in proportion to the relative importance of that objective.

### 1.3.2   *Stimulating Student Progress*

As much as possible, the time given over to classroom testing should provide a rewarding experience. The test should furnish an opportunity for the student to show how well he can handle specific elements of the target language; gone are the days when the teacher designed a test to point up his students' ignorance or lack of application.

Tests should be distinctly announced in advance to permit the student to prepare adequately.

If the student himself is expected to demonstrate his abilities, it is only proper that he should learn as soon as possible after the test how well he did. The test best fulfills its function as a part of the learning process if correct performance is immediately confirmed and errors are pointed out.

The long-range objective of the language course, that is, making a "bilingual" of the student, enabling him to use the new language almost as naturally as his native language, should be reflected in the composition of the classroom tests and quizzes.

1. English should not be used, except in giving directions.
2. Only correct forms should be used, so that the student's ear and eye become accustomed to the language as it is really spoken and written.

3. The specific elements to be tested should be introduced naturally. Contrived sentences that would stump even the native speaker ought to be avoided.

### 1.3.3   *Evaluating Class Achievement*

Through frequent testing the teacher can determine which aspects of the program are presenting difficulties for individual students and for the class as a whole. By analyzing the mistakes made on a given test, or more precisely on given items of that test, the teacher can determine where to concentrate extra class drill and how best to assist each student.

At the same time, testing enables the teacher to discover whether the class objectives are being met. Through tests the teacher can evaluate the effectiveness of a new teaching method, of a different approach to a difficult pattern, or of new materials.

The most familiar role of the classroom test is to furnish an objective evaluation of each student's progress: his attainment of course objectives and his performance in relation to that of his classmates.

## 1.4   TEST VS. QUIZ

Both tests and quizzes play a role in the foreign-language classroom. The distinction between test and quiz is one of dimension and purpose rather than of item content.

The test is announced in advance and covers a specific unit of instruction, be it part of a lesson or several lessons. In reviewing for a test, students pull together the work of several class periods. Classroom tests may be given every two or three weeks—in some cases, every week. Such tests may be constructed to last the entire class period; in this case optimum learning efficiency requires the teacher to return and discuss the corrected test as soon as the class meets again. Some teachers prefer preparing a shorter test so that items may be reviewed rapidly at the end of the same class period.

The essence of the quiz is brevity. In contrast to the test, it may be given unannounced. Frequent quizzes encourage students to devote time regularly to their language study. Moreover, the quiz enables the teacher to acquaint students with types of items that can subsequently be used in tests. Students may be told to expect a quiz every period, although on some days the quiz might be omitted. A written or oral quiz may be given at the end of the period (to highlight work done in class). A regular brief laboratory quiz at the end of the laboratory session can be effective in maintaining student attention during the period.

Individual grades on daily quizzes are not of primary importance. The value of the quiz lies in its positive effect on student learning and the practice it affords in the art of test-taking; such practice helps reduce the negative element of nervousness often affecting performance on longer tests.

The value of the test, on the other hand, lies in the completeness with which it examines the material under study. The relative weight given certain elements or skills should therefore accurately reflect the class objectives. If the test is properly weighted, a student's scores will furnish a numerical evaluation of his familiarity with the material the class has studied.

# CHAPTER TWO
# PREPARING
# THE TEST

All too often tests (and, even more frequently, quizzes) are put together haphazardly shortly before they are to be administered because the teacher is overworked and unable to devote much time or thought to their preparation. In addition, once the tests have been graded they are likely to be forgotten or discarded by the students, for the busy teacher finds even less time to discuss the questions and results with them systematically. Such situations are unfortunate, to say the least.

This chapter will provide suggestions for the establishment of an efficient testing program that will eliminate the deficiencies described above. Since most school systems change textbooks infrequently, the additional work required during the first year will permit a substantial saving of time in subsequent years. Even if different books are introduced later, many of the items, with only minor revisions, can be used with the new texts.

## 2.1 OBJECTIVE TEST ITEMS

Objective test items are designed to elicit specific responses from the student. Since there is only one right answer (or in some rare cases

**9**

two right answers), the scorer can very rapidly mark an item as correct or incorrect. More important, when a group of scorers is reading the same test paper, each of them arrives at the same score. (This agreement is called *scorer reliability.*)

The reliability of objective tests and the increased use of electronic computers have led to widespread acceptance of the machine-scored answer sheet. Objective tests processed in this way have proliferated throughout the United States and have been applied to a broad range of subject matter. The items present the student with four or five options from which he must select the correct answer. Although the scorer reliability of these machine-scored multiple-choice tests is almost perfect (allowance being made for occasional mechanical failure), the validity of each test or each section of the test must be determined separately. Just because a test is "objective," it is not automatically a "good" test. Before using any standardized objective test, the teacher should carefully go over the specifications to determine whether they correspond to his own reasons for giving the test.

Written objective tests have been used for many decades. In the 1920's their application to language instruction was discovered, and the professional journals of the period teem with articles on the "new-type" tests. The "new-type" items include sentence completion (often of the fill-in-the-blank variety), true-false sentences, matching exercises, and writing out of dates and numbers.

### 2.1.1 *Terminology*

Let us define some of the terms used in reference to objective test items. An *item* is an entire "question"; it may be considered a miniature test. The word "item" is preferred because it does not imply the interrogative form; items are not necessarily grammatical questions.

In a multiple-choice item, the *stem* is the initial part: either a partial sentence to be completed, a question, or several statements leading to a question or incomplete phrase. The choices from which the student must select his answer are known as *options, responses,* or *alternatives.* One response is distinctly correct or more suitable than the others. Incorrect responses are called *distractors* and should be so worded that they seem attractive to the uninformed or poorly informed student. If a distractor is so obviously wrong that it is never selected, it plays no useful role in the item and should be eliminated or replaced by a new alternative.

### 2.1.2 *Categories*

Objective test items fall into two main categories: passage items and discrete items. In language items the written passage may be replaced by a visual stimulus.

## 2.1.2a  PASSAGE ITEMS

Passage items, as their name suggests, relate to one paragraph or more, to a poem, or to a conversation. The passage may be printed in the test booklet or recorded and played over a phonograph, tape recorder, or language-laboratory console. The items that accompany the passage should enable the teacher to evaluate how well the student understands what he has just read or heard. An effective passage item should be so constructed that an intelligent bilingual could not arrive at the correct answer without having read or heard the passage. In other words, the student should not be able to answer a passage item merely with common sense and a knowledge of the target language; rather he should demonstrate a specific understanding and application of the information in the passage.

## 2.1.2b  DISCRETE ITEMS

Discrete items stand alone. The most common discrete items are utterly independent of each other, and their order on a given test could be transposed without changing their effectiveness. To obtain greater economy in printing, a series of discrete items employing identical options could be presented as a group.

Here is a sample item in Spanish:

Select the best completion for each of the following sentences. Use the key to indicate your response on the answer sheet.

A. Cuántos
B. Cuántas
C. Cuánto
D. Cuánta

1. ¿——————— dinero tiene Ud?
2. ¿——————— cuentas paga el Sr. González? etc.

Correct responses: C, B.

## 2.1.2c  ITEMS WITH A VISUAL STIMULUS

Language items may be developed around a visual stimulus, such as a map, chart, or picture. The simplest item is the true-false or appropriate-inappropriate item. A calendar or clock may also be used to measure how well the students can handle dates or times in the target language.

## 2.2  THE ANSWER SHEET

Although the prepared answer sheet necessitates a slight investment in paper and the use of a duplicating machine, it more than pays for itself in terms of hours saved. Four copies of the sheet on page 12 can be typed on a single

Name_____

Class_____

Test number_____

| | | | | |
|---|---|---|---|---|
| 1. | A | B | C | D | E |
| 2. | A | B | C | D | E |
| 3. | A | B | C | D | E |
| 4. | A | B | C | D | E |
| 5. | A | B | C | D | E |
| 6. | A | B | C | D | E |
| 7. | A | B | C | D | E |
| 8. | A | B | C | D | E |
| 9. | A | B | C | D | E |
| 10. | A | B | C | D | E |
| 11. | A | B | C | D | E |
| 12. | A | B | C | D | E |
| 13. | A | B | C | D | E |
| 14. | A | B | C | D | E |
| 15. | A | B | C | D | E |
| 16. | A | B | C | D | E |
| 17. | A | B | C | D | E |
| 18. | A | B | C | D | E |
| 19. | A | B | C | D | E |
| 20. | A | B | C | D | E |

| | (2) | (3) | (4) | (5) |
|---|---|---|---|---|
| A____ | 19-20, | 19-20, | 18-20, | 18-20 |
| B____ | 17-18, | 16-18, | 15-17, | 15-17 |
| C____ | 15-16, | 13-15, | 12-14, | 11-14 |
| D____ | 13-14, | 11-12, | 9-11, | 8-10 |
| F____ | 0-12, | 0-10, | 0-8, | 0-7 |

Fig. 1

stencil; then the printed tests can be cut lengthwise into columns with a paper cutter. When taking the test, the student indicates his choice of answer by completely blackening the corresponding letter with a soft pencil. If a student changes a response, the first mark must be completely erased. If two black marks appear for the same question, that question is counted wrong.

The box at the top of each column allows the student to make a note of additional instructions. If A = true and B = false, for example, the student is first told to enter a T in the box above column A and an F in the box above column B. Similarly, if A = past time, B = present time, and C = future time, the student will make the appropriate annotations in columns A, B, and C before taking the test.

In preparing to score the test, the teacher marks the correct answers on his copy of the answer sheet. The blackened letters are punched out with a paper punch. To facilitate placing the grid accurately on each student's answer sheet, the numbers 1 and 20 are also punched out. The bottom part of the grid is cut off. To correct a test, the teacher places the grid over the student answer sheet, counts the number of visible black marks, and enters a check next to the appropriate grade at the bottom of the sheet. The grade is dependent on the number of possible responses. Thus, the only steps required for grading each test are aligning the grid, totaling the visible black marks, and drawing a checkmark. Grades may then be entered directly in the record book.

The suggested grades for the numerical scores take into account only the "guess" factor for a 20-item test. A person with no language training will be able to guess an average of 10 correct responses out of 20 when only two choices are allowed. He would average a score of 6 or 7 out of 20 when given three choices and 5 out of 20 when presented with four choices. To cancel this element of chance, the positive score must be at least three points above the average score obtained through pure guessing. Column 2 on the answer sheet gives the grades for tests with two choices, column 3 is to be used with three choices, and so on.

Some words of caution should be introduced at this point. First, there is nothing sacred about a 20-point quiz; on some days the teacher may wish to include only 15 items, or perhaps only 7 or 8. The same answer sheet would still be used, but the teacher would write the number of correct responses at the bottom of each student quiz. Second, the suggested grade-score correspondences at the bottom of the answer sheet are valid only for quizzes of moderate difficulty. On quizzes that are quite easy, the teacher might prefer to establish a cut-off point, such as 18 on a 20-item quiz, and merely mark the papers as "passing" or "failing." On very difficult quizzes, the teacher would write the number of correct responses at the bottom of the answer sheet and determine an appropriate grade-score scale.

Name *answer grid*
Class *French I*
Test number *11*

| | | | | |
|---|---|---|---|---|
| 1. | A | B | C | D | E |
| 2. | A | B | C | D | E |
| 3. | A | B | C | D | E |
| 4. | A | B | C | D | E |
| 5. | A | B | C | D | E |
| 6. | A | B | C | D | E |
| 7. | A | B | C | D | E |
| 8. | A | B | C | D | E |
| 9. | A | B | C | D | E |
| 10. | A | B | C | D | E |
| 11. | A | B | C | D | E |
| 12. | A | B | C | D | E |
| 13. | A | B | C | D | E |
| 14. | A | B | C | D | E |
| 15. | A | B | C | D | E |
| 16. | A | B | C | D | E |
| 17. | A | B | C | D | E |
| 18. | A | B | C | D | E |
| 19. | A | B | C | D | E |
| 20. | A | B | C | D | E |

Name *answer grid*
Class *French I*
Test number *11*

| | (2) | (3) | (4) | (5) |
|---|---|---|---|---|
| A | 19-20, | 19-20, | 18,20, | 18-20 |
| B | 17-18, | 16-18, | 15-17, | 15-17 |
| C ✓ | 15-16, | 13-15, | 12-14, | 11-14 |
| D | 13-14, | 11-12, | 9-11, | 8-10 |
| F | 0-12, | 0-10, | 0-8, | 0-7 |

FIG. 2

Some teachers have brought up the possibility of cheating. When the answer sheets are used with classroom listening tests, students can sense the movement of pencils. Thus, if the correct response on a four-choice item is B, many students will be marking their sheet while the teacher is reading C and D. The poor student would tend to mark B also, getting that item right for the wrong reasons. This problem can be minimized by asking students not to mark their papers until all options have been read. In the language laboratory, the dividers between booths greatly reduce visual communication between students.

Although it is possible that on a single test a poor student may make enough good guesses to receive a high mark (which in that case would be an unreliable estimation of his ability), the general pattern of daily grades over a period of time can present quite a reliable record of that student's achievement. The validity of this evaluation, however, is *always* dependent on the specific content of the quizzes themselves.

## 2.3 THE ITEM FILE

The purpose of an item file is to enable the teacher to arrange items for easy reference and to allow quicker and more efficient test construction. Each question or item is typed on a file card or piece of paper. The advantage of paper is that it occupies less space, but cards are sturdier and are easier to handle and file.

### 2.3.1 *Cards*

The file cards may be 3 x 5, 4 x 6, or 5 x 8. For long multiple-choice items, the largest card is the most convenient. Plain paper is available in pads of many different sizes, but the 5 x 8 (or 5½ x 8½) is again the most convenient. (Typing paper can be cut in half if desired.) It is often helpful to get cards or paper of different colors to facilitate classification.

### 2.3.2 *Format*

Each card should contain only one item. This allows the teacher to record the results of the item analysis on the back of the card. If the item is used more than once, additional results may also be entered on the card. As the new test is being put together, the cards may be shuffled, thus varying the order of the questions from previous tests (see Figs. 3 and 4). Even very brief items, such as those used for sound-discrimination tests, are best written on separate cards so that they can be easily reassembled to form new tests.

```
                        Spanish Writing Test

Michalski I              Type: completion
Paso 7                   Content: a + el
                         Vocabulary: gimnasio, cafetería (p. 7)



         Juan va a la cafetería y Pepe va ___ gimnasio.




    al
```

*front*

FIG. 3


```
         Date              Errors         Number of papers



    Dec. 8, 1965             7                   28

    Dec. 17, 1965            3                   29
```

*back*

FIG. 4


One may, however, put several short phonology items on one card if all the items concern the same sound (see Fig. 5).

For multiple-choice questions the correct answer can be indicated either on the back of the card or in the lower left-hand corner. The clear visibility of the response (A, B, C, or D) will facilitate arranging the items so that the responses appear in random order.

```
                    Spanish Speaking Test
   Michalski I              Type: reading
   Paso 9                   Content: stress on final syllable



             ¿De dónde es el actor popular?
       Check:              acTOR popuLAR


             ¿Dónde está la estación, por favor?
       Check:              estaCIÓN      faVOR
```

*front*

Fig. 5

### 2.3.3 *Classification*

Each item should carry a triple classification:

1. chapter or unit (structure and vocabulary)
2. knowledge or skill being tested
3. type of item

The chapter or unit may be coded on the left-hand corner of the card; if desired, the type of item (completion, question-answer, etc.) may be identified by color. The specific content may be abbreviated in the right-hand corner (see Figs. 3 and 5). In addition, files may be kept for such categories as listening tests, speaking tests, and so on.

## 2.4   PREPARING THE ITEMS

The key to successful test construction is a clear and precise definition of the objectives involved. Once the course and unit objectives have been considered, the daily quizzes and the final tests can be laid out accordingly.

In an audio-lingual program, most of the emphasis in the elementary course is placed on listening and speaking. Tests in listening and speaking not only help the teacher assess class and individual progress, but also introduce a positive psychological factor for those students (and their parents) who tend not to take seriously a course with no written assignments. Later, as reading and writing are presented, those skills may also become the subjects of frequent short quizzes.

Selecting the type of test to be given is the first step in preparing the items.

One day a week a short listening test may be given at the beginning or end of the hour; in that case the teacher should, a couple of days in advance, prepare a first draft of the script, including a few too many items. The night before the test he should reread and edit the script, making sure that he has used all the structures and vocabulary covered that week and weeding out items that are too easy, too difficult, repetitious, or otherwise inappropriate. (If the textbook is not closely indexed, it is worthwhile to keep a notebook in which idioms are listed and words classified according to parts of speech and to their first occurrence in the book. As the semester progresses, the teacher often discovers that he has a tendency to use certain words again and again and to omit others. If all nouns are listed together, it is a simple matter to choose different direct objects, for example, for various items.)

For the final draft of the test, the items are written on cards. If the teacher plans to read the questions, he may do so directly from the cards. For a language-laboratory test, a tape script must be prepared and the items recorded. If the test requires written cues, they may be written on the blackboard (covered perhaps with a map or wall chart until the appropriate moment), or they may be duplicated in advance.

Once the different quizzes for a specific unit have been prepared, the teacher should check them against the unit outline to make certain that all points in the unit are equally covered and that undue emphasis is not inadvertently being given to particular words, sounds, or structures.

The chapters on the various types of tests will give more specific details on the construction of the different types of items.

## 2.5  ASSEMBLING THE TEST

Once the item file has been established, quizzes can be assembled rapidly. Even before the file is complete, it can be of use in preparing a midterm or final examination. The general procedure is as follows:

The teacher determines the objectives of the test and creates a general plan. Then appropriate items are selected from the file. The teacher can freely take items from the unit under study or from any of the preceding units without having to check back in the course materials to determine whether students have already mastered certain words or phrases.

If desired, special cards could be made, each containing the directions for a specific type of item. Once the items for a quiz have been selected, the two or three appropriate "directions" cards are pulled out. The item cards are then arranged in order of increasing difficulty. The numbers of the questions may be indicated in pencil at the bottom of each card. These pencilled numbers can be erased easily once the results of the item analysis have been entered on the cards.

The teacher should fill out an answer key in advance so that any extremely unbalanced distribution of correct responses can be remedied by shuffling the file cards.

For writing tests, scoring tables should be planned. Anticipated responses to essay test items should be listed together with the appropriate number of points to be given for each part of a directed item or aspect of an essay subject.

For a speaking test, a different kind of scoring sheet is needed. If several questions are to be asked of each student and if different aspects of each response are to be judged, then it is often best to prepare individual scoring sheets. In an informal classroom test, when relatively few questions are to be asked, a single scoring sheet may contain the names of all students, perhaps in random order so that they cannot anticipate their turns.

## 2.6  TEST CONSTRUCTION IN MULTISECTION COURSES

Making comprehensive classroom tests is a highly technical task, demanding both concentration and time. In a department offering several sections of a given course, a common test program may be initiated. The construction of tests can be coordinated in the following ways.

### 2.6.1  *Rotation of Responsibility*

Each teacher assumes responsibility for a specific examination during the year. He plans a tentative outline and asks the other instructors to contribute a specific number of items to each section. He also has charge of editing the script, cutting the stencil, and recording the tape.

### 2.6.2  *Small Committee*

A small committee with a rotating membership prepares the common examinations. Each member either constructs certain portions of the test or contributes items to each portion. The committee also handles the mechanics of test preparation.

### 2.6.3  *One Examiner with Released Time*

In a college department, one professor may be given a lighter teaching load in order to construct semester, and perhaps midterm, examinations. This system is especially effective for unifying the objectives and methods of instruction in first- and second-year language courses.

# CHAPTER THREE
# GIVING
# THE TEST

The classroom test should contribute to the learning process by enabling the student to demonstrate his acquisition of skill rather than impede it either by frightening the student or by presenting him with test items that do not accurately reflect the course objectives. Undoubtedly, the content of a test is most important, but the effective administration of a test is a key factor in its success.

## 3.1  TIMING

The big tests, midterms and finals, are usually scheduled by the administration and pinpointed on the school calendar. The teacher enjoys a certain amount of leeway, however, in planning classroom tests—short quizzes and unit tests.

### 3.1.1  *Elementary Schools*

In elementary school few quizzes and tests are given. Class time is spent almost exclusively developing the listening and speaking skills: songs, short poems, dialogues, oral questions and answers all form an integral part of the instruction. The main contribution of Foreign Languages in the Elementary Schools (FLES) is the development of proper speech habits (pronunciation, intonation, and stress patterns) and of a positive attitude toward language learning. During the first years, testing is of interest primarily to the teacher, helping him to evaluate the effectiveness of certain methods and procedures. When the FLES program has been initiated on a trial basis, the administrators will also be interested in observing student progress in order to assess the effectiveness of the program and its role in the educational process.

Informal testing occurs whenever the teacher requests an individual response from a pupil. Short quizzes teach the pupil what procedures and types of questions will make up the more formal tests. The quizzes can be introduced as games or as opportunities to show off how much has been learned; they should be easy enough so that most pupils perform very well.

The few formal tests of the year should be announced well in advance, and their exact scope should be specified. Only those aspects of the language that have been thoroughly practiced in class should be incorporated into the test. A variety of stimuli such as oral cues, pictures, or situation dialogues may be used. Sufficient examples should be given so that all students are at ease before the test begins; the easiest questions should be given first to allow all students to build up confidence before attacking more difficult items.

### 3.1.2  *Secondary Schools and Colleges*

In secondary schools, and even more in colleges, outside work is required. At first the homework in language classes consists of listening to practice discs or tapes; then reading and written homework are assigned. With a variety of academic subjects and extracurricular activities vying for the student's time, the discipline of daily quizzes often proves effective. Some teachers find that an occasional pop quiz maintains student alertness.

Unit tests should be given distinct advance notice, and the material to be covered should be clearly defined. The test that is given should correspond to its announced description, for students receive satisfaction from having prepared certain material carefully and then having the opportunity to show how well they have learned it. If new material is included in the test, or if sections of the announced material are omitted, the students may become discouraged.

### 3.2  REINFORCING CORRECT RESPONSES

The testing program can become a particularly effective component of the teaching program if the students receive positive reinforcement for their correct responses and good performance. They should also be able to go over a test and profit from their mistakes.

### 3.2.1 *Reinforcement on Quizzes*

Short quizzes lend themselves very well to immediate reinforcement. Whether the quiz is given at the beginning or end of the hour, the teacher should allot a few minutes for a rapid review of the items. On occasion the students may exchange their papers and correct the quizzes themselves, but often this procedure is overly time-consuming. Moreover, the students, even the more conscientious ones, often make errors in grading, and in any case the teacher must go over the papers himself. Generally it is more efficient for the teacher to collect the papers and to review the test orally. On spoken tests those students who have performed poorly may be corrected individually or in a small group after the period; the entire class should not sit idly while one student is being corrected, nor should that student be subjected to the possible humiliation of being corrected at length on his test performance in front of his classmates.

### 3.2.2 *Reinforcement on Tests*

With tests immediate reinforcement becomes more difficult. It is possible to allow ten minutes at the end of the period to go over sections of the test—a practice particularly effective for listening-comprehension tests or for written tests with oral cues. If the test involves primarily the skills of reading and writing, then the students usually profit most from review if they can see their corrected papers. The teacher should therefore make every effort to correct such tests within a day or two and, when the papers have been handed back to the students, to go over the questions that posed particular difficulty. Some teachers have the students rewrite in their entirety the items in which they made errors. If the students are quite sure of the correct responses, such a practice provides desirable reinforcement. However, if the poor students do not understand where and why they made mistakes, they gain nothing from spending additional time on wrong forms; these students would profit more from concentrated drill or homework in the areas in which they are weak.

## 3.3 TESTING IN THE LANGUAGE LABORATORY

Today more and more schools have language laboratories. They vary in size and complexity, yet even the simplest of installations, the listening laboratory, can lend itself to a testing program.

### 3.3.1 *Advantages of Language-Laboratory Tests*

Language laboratory tests possess a high degree of objectivity. All students get the same questions, asked the same way and at the same speed. For the teacher there is the added convenience that all students progress together and finish at the same time. At the college level, make-up tests can be self-administered. The test itself, if given at the end of the laboratory period, can be an incentive to the student to apply himself more seriously to learning the lesson material.

### 3.3.2 *Disadvantages of Language-Laboratory Tests*

The language laboratory does not present the student with a "real-life" situation. Indeed, the artificiality of the classroom becomes even more marked in the laboratory, for the classroom at least has the advantage of offering the oral give-and-take of conversation, and the student's comprehension is helped by gestures and facial expressions.

The language-laboratory test, on the other hand, rather resembles a telephone conversation. It has even been suggested that to facilitate the administration of speaking tests simulated phone booths be installed and the student be given an actual telephone receiver to listen to and speak into. His spoken answers would be recorded by remote control and later corrected by the teacher.[1]

Language-laboratory tests have the additional disadvantage that it is technically difficult to confirm immediately correct answers for multisection classes once the test questions have been administered and the students have recorded their answers. As a solution, the proctor or teacher could post the correct answers for multiple-choice or written tests on a bulletin board close to the exit door. If the test is administered only once, answer sheets could be distributed as soon as the test papers have been collected.

### 3.3.3 *Planning the Language-Laboratory Test*

Since students cannot ask questions or show by a quizzical look that they have not understood, the directions for the language-laboratory test must be extremely clear. It is advisable to read the directions twice. The directions should be in English until the teacher is convinced that even the slowest student will understand instructions in the target language.

The laboratory test is prepared as carefully as other language tests. Once the items have been written, the script is typed in page form and the recording made, preferably by native speakers.

Before giving a major test, the teacher should check the equipment carefully to insure that all students hear the oral cues properly. If a spoken portion of the test is to be recorded, the equipment for this should also be checked.

[1] Nelson Brooks, "Using Tape to Test the Language Skills," *Structural Drill and the Language Laboratory*, Francis W. Gravit and Albert Valdman, eds. (New York: Humanities, 1963), pp. 125–26.

### 3.3.4 *Types of Language-Laboratory Tests*

#### 3.3.4a LISTENING

Listening-comprehension and sound-discrimination tests can be administered very effectively in the language laboratory. If desired, a slide projector, opaque projector, or wall chart can furnish additional visual cues. The students indicate their answers to oral multiple-choice questions on an answer sheet. It is also possible to prepare printed answer booklets in which the students respond either to printed multiple-choice questions and answers or to oral questions and printed responses.

#### 3.3.4b SPEAKING

The speaking test in which students record their responses should be administered only in a laboratory with high-fidelity equipment. Both students and teachers become discouraged when they discover that some machines have not been working properly or that responses were occasionally inaudible.

Cues for the speaking test can be oral, written, or visual. More advanced students may also demonstrate their proficiency by reading aloud; the text is distributed, and the students are given several minutes to prepare the reading before recording it.

Informal speaking tests may be given frequently in the laboratory if the teacher regularly monitors his class (as is usually the case in junior high and secondary schools). The following effective method has been suggested. The first or second time a lesson tape is used the students hear and repeat the confirmations of the drills. A second two-phase tape, which is identical with the first, minus the confirmations, is prepared. This latter tape is used on the last day of the lesson. The teacher tunes in to the various student positions at random and grades student production. Such an informal testing system greatly stimulates better performance in the laboratory.[1]

#### 3.3.4c READING

It is possible to have all students work through a reading test at the same speed by using the laboratory. Each student is given a passage to read silently; after a signal the student is presented with a series of related oral questions on tape to determine how well he understood the text.

#### 3.3.4d WRITING

The laboratory can be used to administer writing tests based on familiar oral material. Dictation, pattern drills requiring written response, and directed paragraphs are all variations that can be adapted for use in the language laboratory. More advanced students can be graded on their ability to take notes on a recorded lecture.

[1] Virginia Cables, "The Language Laboratory, Boon or Bane?" *French Review*, Vol. XXXIX (February 1966), pp. 618–22.

# CHAPTER FOUR
# EVALUATING CLASSROOM TEST RESULTS

All measurement includes units and standards. To say that a book is worth 100 means nothing until the unit or standard of measure is defined (dollars? cents? francs? pesos?). Similarly, to say that a student scored 30 is of no significance until we know the length of the test (30 items or 150 items), how difficult the test was (Is 30 a low score or a high one?), and what material the test covered.

The classroom teacher should be familiar with some very rudimentary concepts of measurement as they are applied to foreign languages. This chapter will define basic terms that are of use in discussing classroom tests and will suggest methods for making a simple analysis of both student scores and tests themselves.[1]

## 4.1 SCORES

The scores on a test are usually calculated in numerical terms. Before converting the scores to

[1] For a more complete statistical treatment of the problems of reliability, norms, and standardization, see Norman E. Gronlund, *Measurement and Evaluation in Teaching* (New York: Macmillan, 1965). See also H. B. Lyman, *Test Scores and What They Mean* (Englewood Cliffs, N.J.: Prentice-Hall, 1963).

letter grades, the teacher must organize this collection of numbers into manageable form. Let us look at the various ways of handling the scores of a hypothetical 90-item test administered to 51 students.

### 4.1.1 *Range*

By finding the highest and lowest scores the teacher can determine the test range. He notes the maximum possible score at the same time. Thus, if the highest score on our hypothetical test is 86 and the lowest 53, the range is from 86 to 53 (or 34) and the maximum possible score is 90.

### 4.1.2 *Distribution*

The distribution of scores can best be visualized by listing all possible scores within the range of the highest and lowest scores achieved and then recording after each score the number of students who achieved it. The score distribution of our hypothetical test looks like this:

```
Distribution chart
  Maximum possible score: 90
        90
        89
        88
        87
        86  /
        85  /
        84
        83  //
        82  /
        81  ///
        80
        79  /
        78  //
        77  ///
        76  /
        75  /
        74
        73
        72  /
        71  //
        70  ////        <——— mean
        69  ///          ——— median
        68  ////
        67  ////
        66  //
        65  ///
        64
        63  //
        62  /
        61  //
        60  /
        59  //
        58
        57  /
        56  /
        54
        53  /
```

FIG. 6

### 4.1.3  *Mean*

The *mean* score of the test is the average score. To calculate the mean, all the scores are added and the sum is divided by the number of papers:

$$(M) \text{ mean} = \frac{\text{sum of the scores}}{\text{number of papers}} = \frac{\Sigma S}{n}$$

In the hypothetical test of 90 items, the mean was calculated to be 70:

$$M = \frac{3570}{51} = 70$$

### 4.1.4  *Median*

The *median* refers to the score obtained by the middle paper of the whole group of tests. On this test the median fell between 68 and 69 because 25 papers scored 68 and lower and 26 papers scored 69 and higher.

### 4.1.5  *Standard Error*

The *standard error* (SE) of a score is a statistical estimate of the variation to be expected in the scores of a test. If the hypothetical test were given a second time, student scores would fluctuate; even if the test were given over and over, the scores would shift somewhat each time.

The following table may be used to obtain a rough estimate of standard error:[1]

| n number of items | SE standard error | Exceptions: regardless of the length of the test, the standard error is: |
|---|---|---|
| < 24 | 2 | |
| 24–47 | 3 | 0 when the score is zero or perfect |
| 48–89 | 4 | 1 when 1-2 points from 0 or 100% |
| 90–109 | 5 | 2 when 3-7 points from 0 or 100% |
| 110–129 | 6 | 3 when 8-15 points from 0 or 100% |
| 130–150 | 7 | |

FIG. 7

If we apply the table to our sample test data, we find that the standard error for a 90-item objective test is 5. Now let us consider the student who scored 72. If the student were to take the test repeatedly under similar conditions

[1] Paul Diederich, *Short-Cut Statistics for Teacher-Made Tests*, Evaluation and Service Series, No. 5 (Princeton: Educational Testing Service, 1960), pp. 30–31. This is a free booklet distributed by ETS.

(and not learn anything by repetition), we could expect to find 68 per cent of his scores within 1 SE, that is, between 67 and 77 (72 ± 5). Moreover, 95 per cent of his scores would fall within 2 SE—between 62 and 82 (72 ± 10). Thus we would have a 95 per cent chance of being correct in assuming that he was inferior in performance to the top four students in the class and better than the bottom eight. We would have a 68 per cent chance of being correct in assuming that the student would do less well than the top eleven students and better than the bottom sixteen students were the test given again. We are much less certain about how this student would perform in comparison with those students who made scores close to his. Fortunately the teacher will be giving other tests in the course of the year and will have many occasions to evaluate the performance of each student.

### 4.1.6  *Standard Deviation*

The *standard deviation* (SD, or $\sigma$), which is an average of the degree to which a group of scores deviates from the mean, enters into a great many statistical formulas. The teacher who feels ill at ease with mathematics can calculate the approximate standard deviation for a test as follows: [1]

$$\text{SD } (\sigma) = \frac{\text{sum of high sixth} - \text{sum of low sixth}}{\text{half the number of students}}$$

On the above sample test, we would proceed in this manner:

One sixth of 51 students is $8\frac{1}{2}$.

The sum of the top $8\frac{1}{2}$ papers (scores of the top 8 papers plus $\frac{1}{2}$ score of the ninth paper) is 701.

The sum of the bottom $8\frac{1}{2}$ scores is 497.

Half the number of students is $\frac{51}{2}$, or $25\frac{1}{2}$.

Hence, $\frac{701 - 497}{25.5} = 8$. The standard deviation of the test is 8.

(The standard deviation is always expressed in rounded-off whole numbers.)

### 4.1.7  *Percentiles and Ranks*

For standardized tests a guide is published that gives the percentile equivalents of raw scores. Often there are several tables, classified according to students' age, years of study, and other factors influencing student performance on a particular test. The percentile equivalent for a given score indicates what per cent of those taking the test scored below that mark. Percentile scores could be calculated for the test we have been discussing. The student who scored 82, for example, is in approximately the ninetieth percentile because 46 out of 51 students (or about 90 per cent) received scores below 82.

[1] Diederich, *op. cit.*, p. 23.

Percentile scores are really not necessary for classroom samples, however. The student scores on class tests may be translated into terms of rank within the class group. Thus the student who scored 82 would be ranked fifth in this hypothetical class of 51.

### 4.1.8  *Letter Grades*

In the classroom, raw scores are generally translated into letter grades. The particular method by which letter grades are assigned will vary from test to test. On a very simple test most students will be expected to make a perfect score. Five mistakes might constitute a failing grade. On longer tests of average difficulty the teacher can assign the letter grades on the distribution chart. Sometimes the scores seem to cluster around certain areas and divide themselves conveniently into letter groups. In any case, the teacher will study the distribution chart and consider the difficulty of the test before determining appropriate grades.

For our hypothetical test, we have indicated three possible ways of assigning letter grades; the actual choice would depend on the teacher's opinion about the difficulty of the test.

Fig. 8

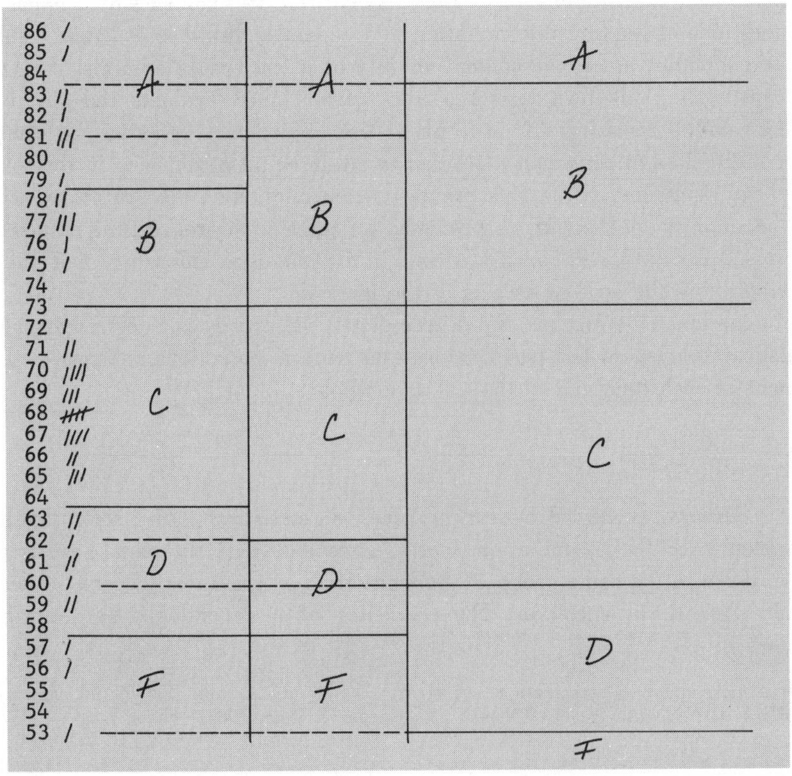

## 4.2 THE CONCEPTS OF VALIDITY AND RELIABILITY

Some tests are poor under any conditions. But even the results of a good test are meaningful only if properly interpreted. The two essential characteristics of a *good* test are:

1. validity (It must measure what it is supposed to measure.)
2. reliability (It must yield a dependable score.)[1]

### 4.2.1 *Validity*

Test *validity*, that is, the relevance of the examination, is the area on which many of the testing controversies have centered: objective tests are criticized for their failure to measure this or that aspect of a subject. The publishers of commercial tests are often at fault for having omitted a detailed description of precisely what the tests presume to evaluate. For example, three different tests may be designated as "first-year Spanish tests," and yet all three may be entirely different: one might be appropriate for use in junior high school, another in senior high school, and a third in college. One might be a listening test with written alternatives for the student to choose from; one might be a reading test with questions in English about Spanish vocabulary and grammar; another might be a written test entirely in Spanish with emphasis on questions of reading interpretation and general cultural knowledge. Thus, the teacher must assess the content validity of a test before administering it. In constructing his own tests too, the teacher must evaluate the validity of the various items in relation to his course objectives. If the teacher wants his college class in elementary German to attain equal proficiency in the four language skills, and if his tests are all written ones, then the test scores will not be *valid* evaluations of his professed objectives. (Moreover, the students, if pressed for time, will spend less time in the language laboratory and more time studying the written aspects of the language.)

For the language teacher, the degree of test validity is not derived from a statistical analysis of test performance, but from a meticulous analysis of the content of each item and of the test as a whole.

### 4.2.2 *Reliability*

Test *reliability*, expressed by test publishers in statistical terms, refers to the consistency of the examination scores. Presumably if the same test were given twice to the same group of students, the performances of each student would show little variation. The requisites of a dependable test are the following:

[1] For a more detailed presentation, see Henry Chauncey and John E. Dobbin, *Testing, Its Place in Education Today* (New York: Harper & Row, 1963), chap. 4.

1. multiple samples
2. standard tasks
3. standard conditions
4. standard scoring

#### 4.2.2a MULTIPLE SAMPLES

For a student's mastery of a complex body of knowledge to be reliably evaluated, he must be asked many questions. He must be given enough opportunities to demonstrate his familiarity with the various aspects of the subject. Learning a foreign language entails not only the acquisition of vocabulary and manipulation of a new grammatical system, but also the mastery of the skills of listening, speaking, reading, and writing. Consequently, a language test, in order to yield a reliable score, must be long enough to provide a generous sampling of the area or areas tested. While the scores on one short quiz cannot be expected to furnish a reliable appraisal of a student's achievement, the average score of a series of quizzes becomes more and more dependable as the number of quizzes increases.

It is also important that there be a wide spread in the level of difficulty of the items. A 75-item test containing items of similar difficulty will be a considerably less sensitive instrument of evaluation than a test of equal length that contains a wide variety of levels of difficulty. The following example will clarify this essential concept:

| Student | Test A (100 items) | Test B (20 items) | Test C (100 items) |
|---------|--------------------|--------------------|--------------------|
| 1 | 97 | 20 | 85 |
| 2 | 92 | 20 | 86 |
| 3 | 80 | 20 | 85 |
| 4 | 73 | 19 | 84 |
| 5 | 66 | 20 | 85 |
| 6 | 60 | 19 | 83 |
| 7 | 52 | 17 | 82 |
| 8 | 43 | 18 | 82 |

FIG. 9

#### 4.2.2b STANDARD TASKS

If the test scores are to provide a dependable means of comparing student performances, then all students must be given the same items or items of equal difficulty. A brief oral test in which each student is asked a different question will yield a reliable score only if each response is scored according to a system that functions independently of the specific content of the items. The concept of standard tasks furnishes the basis for standardized tests: not only are the questions identical (or equivalent), but the format, too, is the same.

### 4.2.2c STANDARD CONDITIONS

The reliability of the test score can be assured only if all the students take the examination under identical conditions. In a listening test, for example, all students must be able to hear the items distinctly. On the individual level, the score of a student who was exhausted or ill at the time of the test will be an unreliable indication of his overall ability.

### 4.2.2d STANDARD SCORING

All tests must be scored in an identical manner. The advantage of multiple-choice tests rests on the fact that a mechanical error is the only element that can lower the dependability of the scoring. The least reliable test scores tend to be those given essay questions. Not only will different teachers disagree about the classification of a group of papers, but an individual teacher, reading the same papers on two different days, may assign different grades to the same essay. Speaking tests also present a scoring problem. Therefore, to obtain a more objective, or reliable, score the teacher should grade each utterance on only one or two specific features, such as fluency or the pronunciation of a recurring vowel.

## 4.3 THE CONCEPT OF CORRELATION

In testing, the correlation coefficient describes the relationship between two series of scores. For example, a *high* correlation exists between two tests if the students scoring high on one generally score high on the other, and if those scoring low on one also generally score low on the other; .89 is a high positive correlation. The correlation is said to be *perfect* if the changes in one score always correspond exactly to a predictable change in the other score; $\pm 1.00$ is a perfect correlation. When the scores on one test correspond in no predictable way to variations of scores on another test, then the correlation is defined as zero. Low correlations range from $\pm.01$ to .30.

The concept of correlation can help the language teacher in two specific areas: determining the relationship between the various language skills and determining the reliability of a specific examination.

Correlation may be represented graphically on a scatter diagram; the pattern of the marks gives the teacher a general idea of the degree of correlation between two variables. Here are some small scatter diagrams: a perfect cor-

perfect positive correlation: 1.00

zero correlation: 0.00

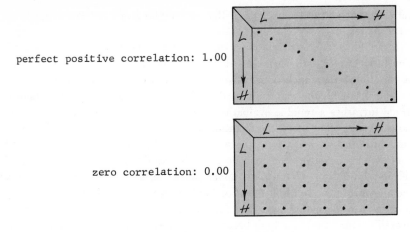

(H = high scores, L = low scores)

Fig. 10

relation is a straight line, whereas zero correlation shows no trace of a grouping of points.

The following chart shows a good positive correlation between the performance on the dictation part of a German examination and the score on the remainder of the examination (listening, reading, and writing). Statisti-

Fig. 11

| Dictation score | Examination score | | | | | | | | | |
|---|---|---|---|---|---|---|---|---|---|---|
| | 40 -49 | 50 -59 | 60 -69 | 70 -79 | 80 -89 | 90 -99 | 100 -109 | 110 -119 | 120 -129 | 130 -139 |
| 11 | | | | / | | | | | | |
| 12 | | / | / | / | / | | | | | |
| 13 | | | / | // | // | | | | | |
| 14 | | | //// | 卌/ | | | | | | |
| 15 | / | / | | // | // | / | / | | | |
| 16 | | | / | 卌 | / | /// | / | | | |
| 17 | | | | //// | /// | 卌 | | | | |
| 18 | | | | / | / | / | //// | /// | / | / |
| 19 | | | | | | /// | //// | 卌// | 卌 | // |
| 20 | | | | | | | | | //// | / |

cally the correlation coefficient of the scatter plot has been evaluated at .90, an extremely high correlation.

Although a good correlation cannot be taken as proof of a causal relationship between two variables, the teacher in the above case could arrive at the following conclusions: given the conditions under which the class had been taught, the materials used, and the skills emphasized, the dictation grade furnishes a reliable evaluation of the student's proficiency in the other skills. On the other hand, the dictation could be suppressed because it changes very little the student's total score on the examination. In arriving at these conclusions, however, the teacher must be cautious not to go beyond the specific limitation of the case under study. It cannot be concluded from the above information that dictation could serve as a complete final examination in any German class. Perhaps the correlation between dictation and overall performance was high because the students were sure they were being graded on a comprehensive two-hour examination; had these students thought that their entire grade would depend on the dictation, they probably would have spent time practicing dictations. Perhaps their score would not have correlated so highly with overall language proficiency under different conditions.

The correlation coefficient may also be employed in the statistical evaluation of the reliability of an examination. Two sets of scores are compared, just as was done for the two parts of the above German test. However, since the reliability coefficient refers to an entire test, statisticians employ various methods to obtain two sets of scores. They may compare the results of one group of students taking the examination twice, or of two similar groups of students taking the same examination, or of two groups taking equivalent versions of the examination. Another way that usually proves more feasible is to compare each student's performance on the even-numbered questions with his performance on the odd-numbered questions (split-half reliability).

For a standardized test, publishers try to attain a minimum reliability of .90. However, not only are classroom tests shorter than most standardized tests; the teacher has little opportunity to pretest items in order to select those that are best. The reliability of a good classroom test generally falls beween .60 and .80.[1]

An estimate of classroom-test reliability may be obtained with the following Kuder-Richardson formula:

$$\text{reliability} = 1 - \frac{M(n - M)}{n\sigma^2}$$

Here $M$ is the mean, $n$ the number of items, and $\sigma$ the standard deviation. Let us refer back to the sample test scores described above (4.1.2) to calculate the reliability of that test.

[1] For a table showing the approximate reliability of tests, see Diederich, *op. cit.*, pp. 30–31.

$M$ (mean; see Section 4.1.3) $= 70$

$n$ (number of items) $= 90$

$\sigma$ (standard deviation; see Section 4.1.6) $= 8$

Hence,

$$\text{reliability} = 1 - \frac{70(90 - 70)}{90 \cdot 8^2}$$

$$= 1 - \frac{70 \cdot 20}{90 \cdot 64}$$

$$= 1 - .243$$

$$= .76$$

## 4.4  RECALL VS. RECOGNITION

Another controversy over standardized objective tests arises from disagreement over the respective roles of recall and recognition in the acquisition and retention of knowledge. When a student must write out an answer or respond to a question orally, he is utilizing his power of *recall;* he must actively remember the necessary facts, forms, or structures before formulating the response. On a reading- or listening-comprehension test, the student can select the correct alternative from the given choices through a process of *recognition;* he might not remember the right answer, but when he sees it printed in the test booklet he passively recognizes it as being appropriate. If the student does not know the answer at all, he will have given an entirely wrong answer on the recall test or leave the question unanswered. On the recognition test the student will be able to guess; moreover, if he is able to eliminate one or two of the options as obviously wrong, he will narrow his margin of error by reducing the number of choices.

In the language classroom the teacher works to develop proficiency in four skills: listening, speaking, reading, and writing. Speaking and writing tests measure the active power of recall; listening and reading measure the power of recognition.

It is possible in some areas to develop *partial production* tests that involve both recall and recognition. The reading skill (recognition) may be used to evaluate certain aspects of speaking and writing (recall). Let us look at two brief examples in English.

The first is a vocabulary item. Given a definition and the first letter of the word defined, the student must think of the complete word and remember how to write it:

A tall building of over thirty stories, such as one sees in Manhattan, is called a (an)

A. a_____.

B. c_____.

C. s_____.

D. t_____.

The correct response is C: skyscraper. Had the student taking the test thought of some combination word beginning with "air," he might have selected A; had he tried to begin the word with "cloud," B would have looked attractive; the word "tall" would have encouraged him to select distractor D.

The second item is one of pronunciation. The student must remember how the words sound before selecting the appropriate response:

Which of the following words does *not* rhyme with the others?

A. could
B. would
C. good
D. food

Correct response: D

In general, recall items are more difficult than recognition items. If the subject matter is the same, the student will obtain a higher score on a 100-item recognition test than on a 100-item recall test, because his passive knowledge of a subject is usually more extensive than his active knowledge. And yet, equivalent recognition and recall vocabulary tests, if well-constructed, both are valid and correlate highly with each other. Nevertheless, scores would in most cases be numerically different for a particular individual.

For foreign-language tests, the degree of correlation between listening tests (recognition) and reading tests (recognition) or between speaking tests (recall) and writing tests (recall) has yet to be established. The language teacher in the classroom should therefore employ a combination of recall, recognition, and partial production tests to evaluate the various facets of language learning.

## 4.5 SPEED TESTS VS. POWER TESTS

Although all tests have some sort of time limit, time is an essential element of some types of tests and not of others. On a *power* test, sufficient time is allowed for even the slowest student to finish, even though he may not actually do so because of the difficulty of the items. In grading a power test (and most classroom tests are power tests), the teacher is interested in seeing how well each student has done, what his total score is, and what grade best describes his performance. If the items are arranged in order of increasing difficulty, then it is not necessary that all students finish; a student's own stopping or slowdown point may be taken as an indication of his proficiency. Even with additional time the student would probably not have improved his performance significantly.

On a *speed* test the student works against time. A typical speed test is the typing test in which the secretary tries to improve her rate of words per minute. On speed tests the level of difficulty remains constant throughout the test. On a language speed test even the better students know that they will probably not be able to finish. Their score will depend not only on knowledge and comprehension but also on the speed at which they progress. In order to discourage indiscriminate guessing on a speed test, the numerical scores are often modified:

two options (for example: true-false)
   adjusted score = number right − number wrong
three options
   adjusted score = number right − ½ number wrong
four options
   adjusted score = number right − ⅓ number wrong
five options
   adjusted score = number right − ¼ number wrong

The rationale of this adjustment is the following. Let us assume that out of 100 items with four options, Student A had finished 60 items when he realized that only thirty seconds remained. He quickly marked Response A for Items 61 through 100 on his answer sheet; he hoped to get about one out of four correct and thus raise his score by 10 points. If we assume that Student A actually did make 10 correct guesses and 30 wrong ones, then his adjusted score on Items 61 to 100 would be

$$10 \text{ right} - \tfrac{1}{3}(30 \text{ wrong}) = 0$$

Thus, Student A gained nothing through his wild guessing.

On the power test, where all students have the time to finish all the items they are capable of doing, such an adjustment is unnecessary. No student would have to answer a long series of items by blind guessing in order to finish the test before the time limit.

## 4.6   ITEM ANALYSIS

An analysis of the responses to the individual items of a test will prove helpful for two reasons. First, the teacher can discover if there are certain points that a sizable number of the students have failed to master. Remedial work may be indicated before proceeding to the next unit. Second, the teacher can verify how well certain items have performed in relation to the test as a whole. This information will be useful in constructing new tests.

Several terms should be clarified. Item *difficulty* is determined by observing what percentage of the students answer the item correctly. The more difficult the item is, the fewer will be the students who select the correct option. *Discriminatory power* tells how well the item performs in separating the better students from the poorer students. If the upper third of the students gets the item correct and the lower two-thirds generally get the item wrong, then it is a good discriminator between these two groups. Very difficult items should discriminate between the very good students and all of the others; relatively easy items should discriminate between the majority of the students in the class and the few poor ones.

### 4.6.1 *Tallying Errors*

For short tests and for tests with two options, the teacher can do a very rapid item analysis by tallying the errors. If errors are marked in red pencil during grading, the teacher can easily find them for transfer to the analysis sheet.

Here is a sample tally chart:

| Subject _Russian I_ | Test number _8_ |
|---|---|
| Class _A_ | Number of papers _31_ |
| Item number or description | Number of errors |
| 1 | //// |
| 2 | -卌 // |
| 3 | // |

FIG. 12

When the results have been tallied, the teacher can see which items proved particularly difficult. A review of the item should be made to determine whether the item itself was faulty (ambiguous wording? poor recording?) or whether the point being tested had not been properly assimilated by the students.

### 4.6.2 *Full Item Analysis: the Entire Sample*

On a multiple-choice objective test administered with answer sheets, the teacher may wish to analyze the performance of the various options. The answer sheets are reviewed one by one, and the student's selected response for each item is transferred to the analysis chart.

Here is a sample item-analysis chart:

| Subject _Spanish I_ | | Test number _12_ | | | |
| Class _9th grade_ | | Number of papers _30_ | | | |

| Item number | Options | | | | Total |
|---|---|---|---|---|---|
| | A | B | C | D | |
| 1 | HH HH HH II | // | HH | HH | 30 |
| 2 | //// | HH HH HH | HH I | HH | 30 |
| 3 | HH HH I | /// | HH HH I | HH | 30 |
| 4 | //// | HH HH HH // | // | HH I | 29 |
| 5 | HH | HH | HH HH //// | HH I | 30 |
| 6 | HH HH HH HH HH HH | | | | 30 |
| 7 | // | /// | // | THT HH HH HH // | 30 |

Fig. 13

Once all the tallies have been entered, the correct answer for each item is circled for rapid identification.

In Figure 13, Items 1, 2, 5, and 7 performed well. The majority of the students selected the correct response, and the remaining tallies are distributed rather evenly over the remaining three options. Item 3 should be reviewed because most of the responses were evenly divided between A and C; perhaps the wording of the item was faulty, or perhaps the item was very difficult and the distractor C represented a common error for American students (indicating the need for more intense drill in class). On Item 4 the majority of the students selected the wrong answer. Was the answer key at fault? Was the item poorly stated? Was an especially tricky point being tested? For Item 6 all the students selected the correct response; this item does not help in discriminating between students and on a subsequent test should be rejected or used as an initial item.

### 4.6.3 *Full Item Analysis: Divided Sample*

When two or more classes have taken the same test, a more informative type of item analysis may be made. First, the answer sheets are arranged in rank order from the highest score to the lowest.

### 4.6.3a DIVISION BY THIRDS

The papers are divided into three piles: the top third, middle third, and bottom third. As each paper is reviewed, the student responses are entered in the appropriate column on the analysis chart. Here is a sample analysis chart:

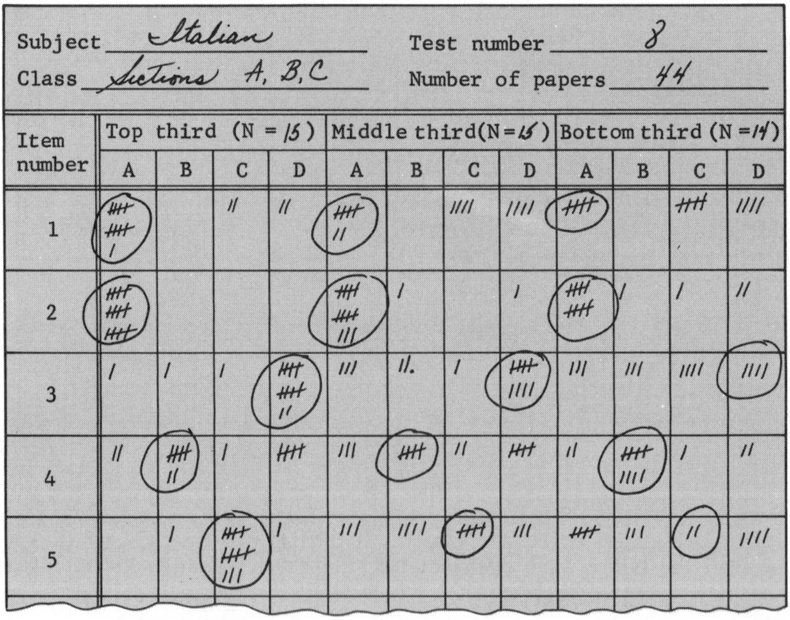

FIG. 14

A good item should exhibit the pattern seen on this chart: the top third shows more correct choices than the middle third, and the middle third shows more than the bottom third. An easy item (Item 2) can be answered by all three groups; if used on another test, it should be the first item. Item 3 discriminates between the middle group and the bottom group. Item 5 is another good item, though more difficult than Item 3; it discriminates between the top group and the middle group. Item 4 should be revised or discarded since it performed negatively: more students in the lowest group answered it correctly than students in the top group. Option B in Item 1 should be revised: it was so obviously a wrong response that it was not an effective distractor.

### 4.6.3b  UPPER 27 PER CENT AND LOWER 27 PER CENT

In a formal statistical item analysis, the upper and lower 27 per cent of the papers are selected and the performances of the two groups compared. A good item discriminates positively between the two groups; for the lower group all the distractors appear relatively attractive. In a formal item analysis the difficulty, the reliability, and the discriminatory power of the test items will be calculated in statistical terms. For the classroom teacher, a visual comparison will immediately provide usable results. Here is a simplified item-analysis chart:

| Subject _German II_  Test number _3_ | | | | | | | |
| Class _all sections_  Number of papers _82_ | | | | | | | |
| Item number | Upper 27% (N = 22) | | | | Lower 27% (N = 22) | | | |
| | A | B | C | D | A | B | C | D |
| 1 | ⦗HH HH HH HH //⦘ | | | | ⦗HH HH HH HH⦘ | / | | / |
| 2 | // | ⦗HH HH HH HH⦘ | | | ///( | ⦗HH HH HH⦘ | / | // |
| 3 | | / | / | ⦗HH HH HH HH⦘ | /// | //// | // | ⦗HH HH ///⦘ |
| 4 | ⦗HH HH HH ///⦘ | / | // | / | ⦗HH //⦘ | HH | //// | HH / |
| 5 | / | ⦗HH HH⦘ | HH HH | / | HH // | ⦗HH⦘ | HH | HH / |
| 6 | //// | //// | ⦗HH HH /⦘ | /// | // | /// | ⦗HH HH HH⦘ // |  |

FIG. 15

Items 1 through 4 are found to have been arranged in order of increasing difficulty; all performed well though Item 1 (answered correctly by all but two students) was particularly easy. Items 5 and 6 should be reviewed for possible faulty wording or ambiguity.

### 4.6.4 *Item Analysis by Show of Hands*

Realizing that the tallying of student scores represents quite an investment in teacher time, Paul Diederich developed the system described in the following sections for carrying out simple item analyses in the classroom.[1]

#### 4.6.4a COUNTING ERRORS

The scored test papers are either returned to their owners or distributed randomly. As the teacher calls out each item number, those students holding a paper with a *wrong* answer raise their hands. For each item the teacher counts the show of hands and enters the figure on his copy of the test. If a sizable percentage of the students answered an item wrong, that item may be discussed later in class. After the first few weeks of instruction, the analysis may be carried out in the target language.

#### 4.6.4b HIGH-LOW ANALYSIS

After scoring the papers, the teacher arranges them in rank order from high to low. The top half of the papers is distributed to one side of the class, the bottom half to the other. If there is an odd number of papers, the responses on the middle paper are not counted in the analysis. The student who holds this middle (or odd) paper is appointed scorekeeper; he records the figures for analysis on the blackboard. He also writes the figures on the odd paper.

This time, as the item number is read, the student will raise his hand only if his paper got the item *right*. One student counts hands for the low group and another counts hands for the high group. As the item analysis proceeds, four figures are recorded for each item:

H   number of highs who answered correctly
L   number of lows who answered correctly
H + L   total number who answered correctly (success)
H − L   how many more highs than lows answered correctly (discrimination)

The teacher or scorekeeper first writes the high and low on the board (as these figures are called out by the two student counters), then mentally calculates and notes H + L and H − L on the board. Each student copies these figures on the test he has before him; the teacher marks them on his copy, and the scorekeeper marks them on the odd test paper.

[1] Diederich, *op. cit.*, pp. 6–12.

For example, on Item 1 the numbers might read:

13     7     20     6

This would mean that 13 in the high group and 7 in the low group answered Item 1 correctly. In all, 20 got the item right (success), and the difference between the groups (discrimination) is 6.

In order to interpret success and discrimination the teacher must take into account the number of students in the class. In the above sample, 28 papers were used. Generally, the most appropriate and most effective items are those answered correctly by 60 to 70 per cent of the class, but on classroom tests this might range from 30 to 90 per cent. A figure under 30 per cent indicates an item is probably too difficult; one over 90 per cent, that it is too easy. On the above test, from 8 to 25 students should have selected the right answer on each item. Discrimination should be above 10 per cent—preferably 15 per cent—of the class; this would mean more than 3 or 4 in the above test. Note: These are statistical evaluations of the item's *performance.* The foreign-language teacher must always remember the importance of the item *content;* only when satisfied that the proper content is being tested should the teacher strive to improve the performance of the item.

When each student gets his own paper back, he can see how well he did on each item in relation to the rest of the class. Students are usually eager to point out poor distractors, ambiguities, and other faults, thus helping the teacher improve the items. In addition, such a classroom item analysis conducted in the target language gives the students excellent practice in handling numbers and carrying out simple arithmetic operations.

On his own, the teacher should look into those items that proved too easy or too difficult and perform a full item analysis on those items with a poor discrimination index.

# PART TWO
# METHODS OF
# EVALUATION

# CHAPTER FIVE
# THE LISTENING
# TEST

Because of the increased emphasis today on direct communication in the foreign language, the skill of listening has become the object of growing attention. Since the majority of the new language programs first introduce listening and speaking, the need for classroom listening tests has arisen. Once the listening skill is considered a course objective, it becomes necessary to assess student achievement in that area.

## 5.1 GENERAL CONSIDERATIONS

What is listening? When a person comments that French and Italian are musical languages or that German and Arabic sound guttural, he almost certainly does not speak those languages. When someone merely "hears" a language spoken, he receives a vague overall impression of new sounds and intonations. This same person would probably be embarrassed when asked to characterize English succinctly because he is unable to "hear" his native tongue with detachment. Instinctively he is "listening"—attaching meaning to the sounds and patterns that strike his ear.

In learning a foreign language, the student

**47**

must acquire the skill of listening. The American, for instance, must learn to differentiate between the sound systems of English and the target language and to discriminate among the unfamiliar sounds of the latter. It is only when he perceives the distinguishing features of the new phonetic system that he can begin to speak the target language accurately. He must rely on his ear both to understand what is being said and to verify his pronunciation.

The skill of listening requires proficiency in three areas: discrimination, retention, and comprehension. Although the native speaker will find listening a natural single operation, the beginning foreign-language student may have to develop proficiency separately in each of the three areas. The teacher may have to measure the student's proficiency in each area or in combined areas.

The native speaker of English automatically makes the necessary sound distinctions in his language. He can recognize those elements or sounds which connote meaning even though he has had no training in phonetics and can give no phonetic analysis of the speech of others. When learning a new language, the American student tries to apply English phonemic [1] differences to the target language. The greatest difficulties arise when the target language uses different sounds, or uses sounds that occur occasionally in English but pass unnoticed because they are not phonemic. German, for example, makes a phonemic distinction between long and short vowels, between a pair of words like *Stadt* and *Staat;* an American can lengthen his vowels voluntarily but needs practice before learning to automatically discriminate vowels phonemically according to length.

In describing phonemic differences of a language, linguists try to find minimal pairs of utterances, that is, ones in which the difference in meaning depends on only one pronunciation feature. In English, *beat* and *bit* (or *he bit him, he beat him*) form a minimal pair that Americans can easily identify but that offers difficulty to speakers of Spanish, French, and other languages which do not possess this distinction. French speakers tend to differentiate between the two words according to vowel length because *beat* is usually longer than *bit;* when the vowel of the latter is consciously lengthened, the American can still distinguish the two words, whereas the Frenchman may become confused. The ability to discriminate the sounds of a foreign language may initially be equated with the ability to distinguish the minimal pairs of the language. Once the student broadens his knowledge of structure and vocabulary, he will be able to rely on context to help him discriminate troublesome phonemes.

---

[1] A *phonemic* contrast is a sound contrast that changes meaning. A *phoneme* is a class of sounds which functions as a unit in the language under study and can be distinguished from other such units. The linguist can show the existence of a given phoneme in a specific language by discovering a *minimal pair*, i.e., two utterances with different meanings but pronunciations in which only one sound feature is varied. For a lengthier discussion of these terms, see Nelson Brooks, *Language and Language Learning*, 2nd ed. (New York: Harcourt, Brace & World, 1964), pp. 275–77.

Native Americans are able to listen to lengthy questions in English and answer with ease. When learning a foreign language, however, these same people can retain only a part of what they have just heard. How often has the teacher seen a student begin to answer a question and then stop to say he has forgotten the final part of the answer or to ask that the question be repeated? Experiments evaluating student ability to remember lists of nonsense words or syllables have shown that those students who impose a certain pattern on the words or syllables increase their retention span. In other words, once students have given a certain meaning to the words, they can remember them more easily. Thus, in the target language, once the student finds himself at ease in the language and understands it with little difficulty, he can retain longer sentences. Retention, which is a serious problem for beginners, seems to present less of an obstacle for the intermediate and advanced students.

In testing retention as such, sentences should be constructed that use words and structures with which all the students are familiar. In this way the teacher can determine whether a poor student needs exercises in memory development or whether his problem is one of vocabulary and grammar. It is generally felt that those who have learned to use a foreign language without reference to English have a longer retention span than those who mentally establish English equivalents.

The main object of a listening test is to evaluate the student's comprehension. His degree of comprehension will depend on his ability to discriminate phonemes, to recognize stress and intonation patterns, and to retain what he has heard. In conversation, however, understanding the target language obviously also requires a knowledge of vocabulary and grammar. A foundation in vocabulary and grammar may be acquired orally, through reading, or through a combination of these methods. A foreigner learning English who is familiar with vocabulary and structure but who possesses only the most rudimentary ideas about pronunciation will easily be able to distinguish between *taking a bus* and *taking a taxi* since *bus* and *taxi* sound considerably different. But this same foreigner may not be able to understand the difference between *Dad is washing the dog outside* and *Dad is watching the dog outside*. If a teacher asks a student to distinguish between *bus* and *taxi* in a listening test, he is using an aural testing method to evaluate the student's knowledge of English vocabulary. If the teacher asks him to distinguish between *washing* and *watching*, he is measuring the student's competency in listening discrimination. Listening discrimination will be more reliably evaluated if the student's knowledge of the two key words has been previously verified by other means, such as a written vocabulary item.

The phenomenon of listening comprehension is quite complex. In conversation a native speaker does not consciously make all the possible phonemic discriminations typical of his language. He is so familiar with certain patterns and contexts that he can understand what is being said even if he does not pay precise attention to every word. To demonstrate this, try the following experiment. Read this paragraph aloud at rapid conversational speed:

> Mr. Jones is driving his car up the driveway. I see he is getting out the hose and a pail of water. And his wife is bringing the rags and sponges and the cleanser for the white sidewalls. But it looks like he's not just going to watch his car; he's planning on waxing it too. A real spring cleanup!

The context in the paragraph is so suggestive that almost all native speakers would assume that you said *wash* rather than *watch*.

A marked comprehension problem for the language student arises from the difference between natural and stylized speech. Newscasters, in particular, employ a highly stylized delivery. Movies and television programs in the target language are often hard to understand. In intermediate and advanced classes taped radio broadcasts and foreign-language films can provide a basis for listening-comprehension tests.

More advanced students can be tested on their comprehension of different types of conversational speech. An American may understand the carefully enunciated French of his teacher and the somewhat deformed French of his classmates. He may even understand when native Frenchmen are talking with him, but conversation between two Frenchmen sounds to him like gibberish. An effort should be made therefore to familiarize advanced students with the variations of the conversational language. For example, in English *jeetjet* looks like nonsense when seen on the printed page, but when read aloud with a rising intonation any American would understand *Did you eat yet?* All languages have a rapid form of speech, used even by cultivated people, that often seems incomprehensible to the foreigner. Excerpts of such speech can serve as the basis of valid comprehension tests.

The order in which the various listening tests described in this chapter are used will depend on the course of instruction. Some teachers emphasize phonemic discrimination from the beginning of the course, while others prefer to establish the general intonation and stress patterns of the dialogues first and to introduce pronunciation drills later. In either classroom situation, appropriate short listening tests are useful from the beginning. Only when the teacher is satisfied that the students hear differences between sounds and intonations can he expect the students to have reasonable success in their efforts to reproduce them. Only when students distinguish between acceptable and unacceptable pronunciation may they be expected to profit from laboratory sessions during which they make and play back recordings of their own voices.

Even teachers who emphasize the skills of reading and writing will find that many of the types of tests described in this chapter may be adapted to their requirements.

## 5.2  LISTENING TESTS FOR FLES AND BEGINNING CLASSES

In FLES (Foreign Languages in the Elementary Schools) programs, as well as in beginning language classes at other levels, emphasis is generally placed on the acquisition of the audio-lingual skills: listening and speaking. If the skills of reading and writing have not yet been introduced, or if these graphic skills are not yet as developed as the audio-lingual skills, the listening test cannot validly be constructed around printed options or questions to be answered in writing. Consequently, listening proficiency is being evaluated with a variety of relatively new testing methods: ABCD items, body-movement, drawing, and picture items.

### 5.2.1  *ABCD Tests*

Older students can be presented with a spoken question and three or four spoken responses from which they are to select the proper answer: A, B, C, or D. Such tests are given with the type of answer sheet described in Section 2.2. These listening tests do introduce an element of retention, for the student must remember the stem he has just heard as well as the possible responses. For FLES students, such items must contain very brief options in order to be effective:

Snow is    A. blue.
           B. white.
           C. red.
           D. orange.

Correct response: B

### 5.2.2.  *Body-Movement Tests*

Listening comprehension may be assessed by asking the student to carry out specific instructions, such as raising his left hand or opening his book. Body-movement tests are more practical in the freer, more mobile atmosphere of the elementary school. Such tests do have their limitations. If the entire class is asked to perform a task, such as standing up, the poorer students will imitate the better ones. If each student is given a different order to carry out, the test is not extremely reliable because each student is tested on different vocabulary items and on only one or two tasks. Moreover, the test is quite time-consuming. Finally, the vocabulary and grammar that can be tested in this way are limited.

### 5.2.3 *Drawing Tests*

In FLES classes crayon tests, in which the student colors or draws certain pictures, may be used in testing knowledge of forms, numbers, objects, and colors. With older students, pencil-and-paper tests are usually limited to the following item types (which are also effective with FLES classes): telling time by drawing in the hands of a clock, indicating dates on a blank calendar, writing down dates and times, and carrying out arithmetical operations of varying degrees of complexity. (Since the writing of digits cannot really be considered part of the writing skill, such items have been classified as "drawing" tests.)

### 5.2.4 *Picture Tests*

The potential of picture tests in language classes has not yet been fully exploited; the possibilities are many, even for the teacher who does not feel artistically gifted. Magazine pictures, cut out and mounted on cardboard, can be shown to the class while the items are being read. Care, of course, must be taken in their selection in order to avoid ambiguous interpretations.

#### 5.2.4a DISCRETE PICTURE ITEMS

Each spoken item is accompanied by one or more pictures. If one picture is used, the item is of the true-false or the appropriate-inappropriate type:

This is a tree.

Correct response: true

Several pictures may be used for one item:

The boy is running.

Correct response: A

A      B      C

In a more sophisticated form, this type of item forms the basis of the Common Concepts Test (see Appendix).

#### 5.2.4b PICTURE "PASSAGE" ITEMS

When possible, it saves time to select a picture or pictures that can be used with several items. A domestic scene, for example, can be accompanied by a list of descriptive sentences to be marked true or false. A more reliable test, and the most versatile of this type, uses a series of four or five pictures representing different situations. On hearing a descriptive statement, the student marks the letter corresponding to the proper picture. Short dialogues can be recorded and the student asked to indicate the pictorial situation in which such a conversation would most likely occur.

## 5.3 DISCRIMINATION OF SOUNDS

In acquiring proficiency in the target language, the student must learn to discriminate among the phonemes of the new language and to differentiate between the distinctive phonetic features of English and those of the target language.[1] This ability may be assessed most rapidly through the use of multiple-choice objective tests.

Note: The items described in Sections 5.3.1 and 5.3.2 measure sound discrimination in isolation. Such techniques, while providing an excellent means of judging progress in phonetics classes, are not always suitable for beginning students. Since the emphasis in audio-lingual classes is on direct oral communication, the ability to discriminate among sounds is best assessed as a function of the meaning transmitted by those sounds (see Sections 5.3.3 and 5.3.4).

### 5.3.1 *Sounds: English vs. Target Language*

Not all sounds in the target language need to be tested. Those sounds nearly identical in pronunciation and distribution in both languages present no great learning problem. The general areas of probable interference between the two languages are the following:[2]

vowel substitution: English MAN /mæn/
German man /man/
vowel glide: English SAY /sei/
Spanish sé /se/
consonant articulation: English MET/mɛt/ (alveolar [t], often unreleased)
French mette /mɛt/ (dental [t], strong release)

---

[1] Consult the Contrastive Structure Series, ed. Charles A. Ferguson (Chicago: University of Chicago Press). The series includes: William G. Moulton, *The Sounds of English and German* (1962); Frederick B. Agard and Robert J. Di Pietro, *The Sounds of English and Italian* (1965); Robert P. Stockwell and J. Donald Bowen, *The Sounds of English and Spanish* (1965). These studies describe the similarities and differences between English and the five languages commonly taught in the United States: French, German, Italian, Russian, and Spanish.

[2] English words will be printed in capital letters.

In order to determine the student's sensitivity to these areas of possible interference, the student is asked either implicitly or explicitly to compare his native English with the target language. When told to pick out the English words, some students begin considering the wide variety of American dialects and realize that they can understand English spoken with a broad range of foreign accents. Thus, if the student is requested to pick out which words of a series belong to one of the languages, it appears preferable to ask him to select the words that he considers typical of the target language. In implicit contrast items, students are asked to indicate whether the words they hear are identical or different.[1]

### 5.3.1a SAME VS. DIFFERENT: TWO WORDS

You will hear two words. Listen to determine whether the two words are the same or different. Indicate your answer as follows: A = $\boxed{\text{same}}$, B = $\boxed{\text{different}}$.

Here is a sample item for Italian:

il EEL

Correct response: B

### 5.3.1b SAME VS. DIFFERENT: THREE WORDS

You will hear three words. Indicate which word in the group is different.

Here is a sample item for French:

A. gai B. gai C. GAY

Correct response: C

This item may be made more difficult by adding the following instruction: If all three are different, mark D; if all three are the same, mark E. Note: The teacher must make sure that the increased difficulty of the item is *not* due to the increased complexity of the instructions.

### 5.3.1c SAME VS. DIFFERENT: DIRECTED COMPARISON

You will hear one word. After a slight pause you will hear three (or four or five) words. Indicate which of the three (or four or five) words is exactly the same as the initial word.

---

[1] In his work with same-different Spanish tests, Eugène Brière found that items in which the words to be compared were different proved twice as effective as those in which all words were the same (paper read at the annual MLA meeting, Chicago, December 1965).

Here is a sample item for German:

Dach    A. DOCK  B. DOCK  C. Dach

Correct response: C

This item may be made more difficult by adding the following instruction: If none of the three words is the same as the initial word, mark D on your answer sheet; if all three are the same, mark E. However, the teacher must be certain that the directions do not become too complex for the level of the class.

### 5.3.1d  SAME VS. DIFFERENT: MULTIPLE VERSION

You will hear one word. After a slight pause you will hear two more words. Decide whether either or both of the two words are exactly the same as the first word. Indicate your answer as follows:

A. Only word 1 is the same as the first word. | 1 |

B. Only word 2 is the same as the first word. | 2 |

C. Both words 1 and 2 are the same as the first word. | 1+2 |

D. Neither word is the same as the first word. | 0 |

Here is a sample item for French:

SANK    1. SANK  2. cinq

Correct response: A

### 5.3.1e  SAME VS. DIFFERENT: COMPLEX VERSION

You will hear three words or phrases. Listen to determine whether any two or three words (or phrases) are the same. Indicate your answer as follows:

A. Only words 1 and 2 are the same. | 1+2 |

B. Only words 1 and 3 are the same. | 1+3 |

C. Only words 2 and 3 are the same. | 2+3 |

D. Words 1, 2, and 3 are all the same. | 1, 2, 3 |

E. None of the words are the same. | 0 |

Here is a sample item for Spanish:

1. tres  2. tres  3. TRACE

Correct response: A

### 5.3.1f TARGET LANGUAGE VS. ENGLISH: PAIRS

You will hear two words. Indicate which word of the pair is German (insert name of target language).

Here is a sample item:

A. Vieh   B. FEE

Correct response: A

### 5.3.1g TARGET LANGUAGE VS. ENGLISH: COUNTING

You will hear a series of three similar-sounding words. Some may be French (target language); some may be English. Count how many of the words are French. Indicate your answer as follows:

| | |
|---|---|
| A. Only one (1) is French. | 1 |
| B. Only two (2) are French. | 2 |
| C. All three (3) are French. | 3 |
| D. None are French. | 0 |

Here is a sample item:

TWO   tout   tout

Correct response: B

In this type of item the options may be increased by using a series of four words. There would be three new options:

| | |
|---|---|
| C. Only three (3) are French. | 3 |
| D. All four (4) are French. | 4 |
| E. None are French. | 0 |

### 5.3.1h TARGET LANGUAGE VS. ENGLISH: MULTIPLE VERSION

You will hear a series of four words. For each Spanish (target language) word, mark the corresponding space on your answer sheet. You may have to mark more than one space per item.

Here is a sample item:

A. que   B. que   C. KAY   D. que

Correct response: A, B, D

### 5.3.1i TARGET LANGUAGE VS. ENGLISH: COMPLEX VERSION

You will hear two words. Listen carefully to determine whether the words are Italian (target language) or English. Indicate your answer as follows:

A. Only word 1 is Italian.
B. Only word 2 is Italian.
C. Both words 1 and 2 are Italian.
D. Neither word is Italian.

Here is a sample item:

1. LEE   2. LEE

Correct response: **D**

### 5.3.2   *Sounds: Phonemes in the Target Language*

Generally, the target language makes phonemic contrasts that do not exist in English. Invariably, the target language possesses phonemes that have no counterpart at all in English. Recognition of these phonemic differences must precede, or at least accompany, the assigning of lexical or grammatical meaning to these sounds.

Pure discrimination tests, especially those used with beginning students, are usually content-free; that is, the student can select the correct answer without understanding the meanings of the words used. The items are constructed around minimal pairs, utterances in which only the element under study changes. Vowels and final consonant contrasts may be effectively incorporated into an item that requires the student to select perfect rhymes. The ability to make finer contrasts, or contrasts that do not occur in stressed position, is best evaluated through same-different items.

#### 5.3.2a   RHYME: TWO WORDS

You will hear two words. Listen to determine whether the two words rhyme perfectly with each other. Indicate your answer as follows: A = | rhyme |, B = | no rhyme |.

Here is a sample item in German:

fuhr   für

Correct response: B

#### 5.3.2b   RHYME: THREE WORDS

You will hear three words. Listen to determine which word does *not* rhyme with the others and mark the corresponding letter.

Here is a sample item in German:

A. Vater   B. Vetter   C. Kater

Correct response: B

### 5.3.2c  RHYME: DIRECTED COMPARISON

You will hear one word. After a slight pause you will hear three (or four or five) more words. Indicate which of the three (or four or five) words rhymes with the initial word.

Here is a sample item in English:

Set    A. fit   B. seat   C. bet

Correct response: C

This type of item may be made more difficult by adding the following instruction: If none of the three (or four or five) words rhymes with the initial word, mark D on your answer sheet. Again the teacher must make sure that the instructions are not too complex for the level of the class.

### 5.3.2d  RHYME: MULTIPLE VERSION

The voice on the tape will speak one word. After a slight pause you will hear two more words. Listen to determine whether either or both of the words rhyme with the first word, and indicate your answer as follows:

| | |
|---|---|
| A. Word 1 rhymes with the first word. | 1 |
| B. Word 2 rhymes with the first word. | 2 |
| C. Both words 1 and 2 rhyme with the first word. | 1 + 2 |
| D. Neither word rhymes with the first word. | 0 |

Here is a sample item in Italian:

Sposa    1. cosa   2. sposi

Correct response: A

### 5.3.2e  RHYME: COMPLEX VERSION

You will hear three words. Listen to determine whether any of the words rhymes with another or whether they all rhyme or none rhyme. Indicate your answer as follows:

| | |
|---|---|
| A. Words 1 and 2 rhyme. | 1 + 2 |
| B. Words 1 and 3 rhyme. | 1 + 3 |
| C. Words 2 and 3 rhyme. | 2 + 3 |
| D. Words 1, 2, and 3 all rhyme. | 1, 2, 3 |
| E. None of the words rhyme. | 0 |

Here is a sample item in Spanish:

　1. van　2. dan　3. pan

Correct response: D

**5.3.2f**　SAME VS. DIFFERENT: TWO WORDS

See item type 5.3.1a.

**5.3.2g**　SAME VS. DIFFERENT: THREE WORDS

See item type 5.3.1b.

**5.3.2h**　SAME VS. DIFFERENT: DIRECTED COMPARISON

See item type 5.3.1c.

**5.3.2i**　SAME VS. DIFFERENT: MULTIPLE VERSION

See item type 5.3.1d.

**5.3.2j**　SAME VS. DIFFERENT: COMPLEX VERSION

See item type 5.3.1e.

**5.3.2k**　THREE-SYLLABLE WORDS OR PHRASES

You will hear a word or phrase of three syllables. Listen carefully to determine which, if any, of the three vowel sounds are the same. Indicate your answer as follows:

| | |
|---|---|
| A. In syllables 1 and 2 the vowel sounds are the same. | $1+2$ |
| B. In syllables 1 and 3 the vowel sounds are the same. | $1+3$ |
| C. In syllables 2 and 3 the vowel sounds are the same. | $2+3$ |
| D. In syllables 1, 2, and 3 the vowel sounds are the same. | $1, 2, 3$ |
| E. The vowel sounds of the three syllables are all different. | $O$ |

Here are two sample items in French:

　pas du tout

Correct response: E

　tout d'un coup

Correct response: B

In testing the discriminatory ability of more advanced students, the teacher should use unfamiliar words or phrases. If common phrases are used, the students might well arrive at the proper answer by recalling the spelling of the words.

### 5.3.3   *Discrimination of Sounds: Vocabulary*

For intermediate and advanced students sound-discrimination tests may incorporate known vocabulary. The contrast in sound between a pair of utterances distinguishes the meaning of those utterances. Vocabulary-discrimination tests offer a learning incentive because students realize that the ability to differentiate between minimal pairs may be crucial in understanding the target language. For such tests the students should be quite familiar with the words being contrasted so that the only element determining their choice is one of sound-discrimination.

#### 5.3.3a   KEY WORD PLUS PICTURE

You will hear two (or three) words. On your answer sheet indicate which word corresponds to the picture in your booklet (on the board, etc.).

Here is a sample item in French:

A. poison   B. poisson

Correct response: B

To place the word being tested in a more natural context, such utterances may be used as:

A. Voici du poison.   B. Voici du poisson.

or: A. L'enfant mange du poison.   B. L'enfant mange du poisson.

#### 5.3.3b   KEY WORD PLUS PICTURES

You will hear a word or sentence. Look at the pictures in your test booklet (on the board, etc.) and select the one corresponding to the utterance you have just heard.

Here is a sample item in German (based on the minimal pair *Kirche* and *Kirsche*):

Ich sehe die Kirsche (*or* Das ist die Kirsche).

Correct response: B

A          B

**5.3.3c** COMPLETION ITEMS: EXPLICIT DISCRIMINATION

You will hear a single sentence, followed by sentences A and B (and C). Choose the sentence that best completes the idea expressed in the initial sentence.

Here is a sample item in French. (The explicit contrast is between *monte* and *mente*.)

Il doit toujours dire la vérité.

A. Je ne veux pas qu'il monte.
B. Je ne veux pas qu'il mente.

Correct response: B

**5.3.3d** COMPLETION ITEMS: IMPLICIT DISCRIMINATION

You will hear a single sentence, followed by sentences A and B (and C). Choose the sentence that best completes the idea expressed in the initial sentence.

Here is a sample item in French. (The implicit contrast is between *au-dessus* and *au-dessous*.)

Nous habitons au troisième et les Dupont habitent au-dessus.

A. Alors l'appartement des Dupont est au second.
B. Alors l'appartement des Dupont est au quatrième.

Correct response: B

**5.3.4** *Discrimination of Sounds: Structure*

In most languages, certain phonemic distinctions are of morphological importance. The change in a single sound may change the meaning of the grammatical structure. The particular areas tested in a sound-discrimination test will vary from language to language. In this section the sample items will be in French.

**5.3.4a** VERB FORMS

You will hear a sentence once. Listen carefully to determine whether the subject and verb are singular or plural. Indicate your answer as follows:

A. singular
B. plural
C. could be singular or plural

Here are some sample items:

1. Il vient maintenant.
2. Ils acceptent notre offre.
3. Elle(s) le cherche(nt).

Correct responses: A, B, C

### 5.3.4b ARTICLES

You will hear a sentence. Listen carefully to determine whether the last word is masculine singular, feminine singular, or plural. Indicate your answer as follows:

A. masculine singular
B. feminine singular
C. plural

Here are some sample items:

1. J'aime la table.
2. Je n'aime pas les chaises.
3. Je prends le fauteuil.

Correct responses: B, C, A

Items of this type might well employ vocabulary not yet studied; then sound discrimination and not familiarity with a given word would form the basis of choice. The vocabulary element may even be eliminated entirely by asking the student to identify the gender and number of direct object pronouns.

You will hear a sentence once. Listen carefully to determine whether the object is masculine singular, feminine singular, or plural. Indicate your answers as follows:

A. masculine singular
B. feminine singular
C. plural

Here are some sample items:

1. Je la vends.
2. Je le prends.
3. Je les veux.

Correct responses: B, A, C

### 5.3.4c VERB TENSES

You will hear a sentence once. Listen carefully to determine whether the verb is used in the present or the imperfect tense. (Or: Listen carefully to determine whether the action described occurred in the past or is taking place at present.) Indicate your answer as follows:

A. present
B. imperfect (past)

Here are some sample items:

1. Cherche-t-il?
2. Nous finissions le devoir.
3. Vous alliez là-bas.

Correct responses: A, B, B

Note: All the examples above incorporate minimal-pair contrasts. This explains the use of the interrogative form in the first sentence: *cherche-t-il* /ʃɛrʃətil/ and *cherchait-il* /ʃɛrʃetil/ both have the same number of syllables, whereas *je cherche* /ʒəʃɛrʃ/ and *je cherchais* /ʒəʃɛrʃe, ʒəʃɛrʃɛ/ do not.


## 5.4 INTONATION TESTS

Since English uses a rich variety of intonation patterns, most American students learning a foreign language are sensitive to such distinctions. For example, in English the declarative sentence *You're coming* may be transformed into the question *You're coming?* when spoken with a rising intonation. Consequently, most American students can easily identify the same pattern in French: *Tu viens?* In many instances, however, the target language uses intonation patterns that have no English counterpart or that have a different effect than they have when used in English. An intonation pattern suggesting cheerfulness in English may have a cool or impolite tone in Italian (see example in Section 5.4.3).

The students' ability to pick out these differences in intonation may be assessed through tests incorporating the following item types.


### 5.4.1 *Discrimination: Same vs. Different*

Item types 5.3.1a through 5.3.1e may be modified so that students compare intonation patterns. Students will find it easier to compare the intonations of two identical sentences than of sentences using different words.


### 5.4.2 *Linear Representation*

You will hear a sentence. Choose the linear pattern that most closely depicts the intonation curve of the sentence.

Here is a sample item in French:

Qui est là?

A. 

B. 

C. 

Correct response: A

### 5.4.3 *Meaning*

You will hear a sentence. Read the choices given in your answer booklet and choose the most accurate interpretation of the sentence you have just heard.

Here is a sample item in Italian:

Buon giorno. (spoken: )

A. Good morning! (cheerful)
B. Good morning! (Well, you finally got up!)

Correct response: B

Note: In this type of item the reading and vocabulary factors can most easily be eliminated by having the options appear in the students' native language, in this case English.

## 5.5 STRESS AND ACCENT TESTS

Since in English stress is usually indicated by loudness and a rise in pitch, American students experience little difficulty in recognizing stressed syllables if the target language handles them in the same way. Conflict occurs when the target language uses stress to signal distinctions not made in English. When the target language employs very few stress patterns, the American student must unlearn the habits of his native language; these habits are primarily an obstacle to speaking, however, rather than to listening.

In teaching a foreign language, the teacher will want to evaluate the students' ability to discriminate between stress patterns and to interpret them properly.

### 5.5.1 *Discrimination: Same vs. Different*

Item types 5.3.1a through 5.3.1e may be used here. Students are asked to distinguish between minimal pairs, such as *con'vert* and *convert'* in English or *portabagagli* (baggage carrier) and *porta bagagli* (he carries baggage) in Italian.

### 5.5.2  *Written Representation*

You will hear a sentence once. In your answer booklet you will see the sentence transcribed two (or three or four) ways. Capital letters are used to indicate the stressed syllable. Select the transcription that describes the sentence you have just heard and mark the corresponding space on your answer sheet.

Here is a sample item in German:

Er kauft NUR einen Hund.

    A.  Er kauft NUR einen Hund.
    B.  Er kauft nur EINen Hund.

Correct response: A

### 5.5.3  *Meaning*

You will hear a sentence once. In your answer booklet you will see two (or three or four) interpretations of the sentence. Select the phrase which best describes the sentence you have just heard and mark the corresponding space on your answer sheet.

Here is a sample item in Spanish:

Sí, ésta.

    A.  Yes, this one.
    B.  Yes, he is.

Correct response: A

The options may be given in Spanish if the teacher is certain that no comprehension problem exists for the students.

## 5.6  RETENTION TESTS

Occasionally the teacher will want to assess his students' foreign-language retention. Since retention ability has not yet been proven directly proportional to comprehension, the retention test is often considered diagnostic from the teacher's point of view.

It is best to arrange retention-test items in order of increasing difficulty; here difficulty is proportionate to sentence length and to the position of the changing element. Short sentences are naturally easier to remember than long ones; in sentences of equal length, most students have less difficulty spotting a variation toward the beginning of the sentence than near the end. Since retention, rather than sound discrimination, should be evaluated, the choices offered should be based on more than minimal-pair distinctions.

As a control, the teacher might wish to make up a similar retention test in English. A comparison of results would show the differences in retention ability among students with respect to their native language and would permit correlation between their performances in English and those in the target language.

In both English- and target-language tests, the sentences in the items should be read with identical intonation and stress.

### 5.6.1 Same vs. Different: Pairs

You will hear two sentences. Listen carefully to determine whether the sentences are the same or different. Indicate your answer as follows:

A = | same |, B = | different |.

If the test is given for diagnostic purposes, the directions may be modified to include "not sure." The presence of such an option will eliminate the guess factor. The test will discriminate between those who thought they remembered (but were wrong) and those who realized that they did not remember.

Here are some sample items in French:

1. Je viens demain.
   Il vient demain.
2. Jean part à deux heures.
   Jean part à trois heures.
3. Si j'avais mille dollars, je m'achèterais une voiture.
   Si j'avais mille dollars, je m'achèterais une auto.
4. J'espère faire la connaissance de mon cousin français cet hiver.
   J'espère faire la connaissance de mon cousin français cet hiver.

Correct responses: B, B, B, A

Note: Item types 5.2.1b through 5.2.1e could be adapted to this kind of test.

### 5.6.2 Same vs. Different: Comparison

You will hear one sentence followed by three sentences. Mark which of the three sentences is the same as the first.

Here are two sample items in Spanish:

1. ¿De dónde eres tú?    A. ¿De dónde eres tú?
                                    B. ¿De dónde es él?
                                    C. ¿De dónde es ella?

2. Son las dos y veinte.    A. Son las diez y veinte.
                                    B. Son las dos y veinte.
                                    C. Son las dos y cinco.

Correct responses: A, B

## 5.7   LISTENING COMPREHENSION: VOCABULARY

The ability to understand the target language greatly depends on one's knowledge of vocabulary—vocabulary in the broadest sense. Many commercial listening tests may be termed modified vocabulary tests since the correct response to most of the items hinges on one or two cue-words which, if understood, elicit the correct answer. Such listening tests, however, are much superior to traditional written or oral "vocabulary tests" because the lexical items are presented naturally; the student must pay careful attention in order to determine which are the key words and how they are being used.

Since classroom tests should contribute to the learning process, no incorrect forms appear in the items. The student's ear should become accustomed to correct, natural speech. Consequently, vocabulary to be tested should be introduced in a natural conversational framework. A wide variety of oral quizzes may be adapted so that they assess primarily the students' comprehension of key lexical terms.

### 5.7.1   *Listening Comprehension and Body Movement*

Younger students, particularly those in elementary school, enjoy informal body-motion tests of listening comprehension. The following may be used as games or as informal tests. In the latter case, the teacher discreetly evaluates the performance of each student. It is generally advisable not to eliminate students, since those who make mistakes are the ones in greatest need of practice.

#### 5.7.1a   SIMPLE COMMANDS

Each student is told to perform an action. In French, for example, the teacher might suggest:

Robert, lève la main droite.
Marie, va au tableau.

### 5.7.1b DISCRIMINATION OF COMMANDS

The students individually or in groups are told to perform an action. When the teacher fails to use a command form, the students are not to respond. Those who react inappropriately to a sentence are sent to the back of the group. They continue playing and benefit from observing the students in front of them. The winner is the student standing at the front of the group at the end of the test. In Spanish the teacher might suggest:

Levántese Ud.
Siéntese Ud.
Abran Uds. los libros.
Tengo un lápiz.

### 5.7.1c "SIMON SAYS"

This game may be adapted to the language classroom. Only actions preceded by "Simon says" (*Pierrot dit, Siegfried sagt, Pablo dice,* etc.) are to be performed. Students who react inappropriately are sent to the back of the group. The winner is the student left standing in front. In French the game might proceed as follows:

Pierrot dit: Levez la main gauche.
Pierrot dit: Touchez votre nez.
Pierrot dit: Mettez les mains sur les genoux.
Levez la main droite.
Pierrot dit: Fermez les yeux.

### 5.7.2 *Listening Comprehension and Drawing*

Elementary-school students perform well on drawing tests. Students may use pencils or crayons if color is used in the instructions. A short quiz might be composed of four or five pictures. Here are samples in French.

### 5.7.2a SIMPLE VERSION

Dessinez une fleur (rose).
Dessinez un cercle (bleu).

### 5.7.2b COMPLEX VERSION

Dessinez une fleur rose si vous êtes une fille, une fleur pourpre si vous êtes un garçon.
Dessinez un cercle bleu si votre nom commence avec une voyelle, un cercle jaune si votre nom commence avec une consonne.
Dessinez une étoile verte si vous portez des chaussettes blanches, une étoile orange si vos chaussettes ne sont pas blanches.

### 5.7.3  *Comprehension Ease*

One of the goals of an audio-lingual approach to language teaching is enabling the students to "think" in the target language, to understand what is said without having to make a mental translation into English. Listening-comprehension items, based on familiar vocabulary and known structures, can be employed to measure the ease with which a student follows a conversation in the target language. The items are read quite rapidly and are not repeated. Because of the speed element, students for whom the lexical items have acquired a meaning independent of their English equivalents will perform better on this type of test than students less familiar with the vocabulary. On these tests items should be arranged in order of increasing difficulty in order not to discourage weaker students from the outset.

#### 5.7.3a  TRUE-FALSE: VERBAL

You will hear a sentence read only once. Decide whether the sentence is true or false. Indicate your answer as follows: A = $\boxed{\text{true}}$ , B = $\boxed{\text{false}}$ .

Here are two sample items in Italian:

1. La neve è bianca.
2. I colori della bandiera americana sono rosso, bianco, e verde.

Correct responses: A, B

#### 5.7.3b  TRUE-FALSE: PICTURES

(A large picture is held up in front of the class. The teacher may wish to use a pointer to accompany the reading of the sentences.)

You will hear a series of sentences that refer to the picture. Decide whether each sentence is true or false according to the picture. Indicate your answer as follows: A = $\boxed{\text{true}}$ , B = $\boxed{\text{false}}$ .

Here is a sample series in German:

Hier ist eine Uhr.
Sie ist blau.
Es ist jetzt neun Uhr.
Ein Kind kommt in das Zimmer.
Es ist ein Mädchen.

**5.7.3c** TELLING TIME

(A clock with movable hands is used to indicate the time.)

You will hear three sentences. Select the sentence that accurately expresses the time shown on the clock.

Here is a sample item for German:

The clock shows 2:45.    A. Es ist Viertel zwei.
                         B. Es ist Viertel drei.
                         C. Es ist drei Viertel drei.

Correct response: C

**5.7.3d** NUMBERS

(Large flash cards are prepared with numbers, simple arithmetical operations, or dates.)

You will hear three (or four) numbers read. Select the number that accurately expresses what is indicated on the flash card and mark the corresponding letter on your answer sheet.

Here are some sample items for German:

1. Card: 1742    A. tausendsiebenhundertzweiundvierzig
                 B. tausendsiebenhundertvierundzwanzig
                 C. siebentausendzweihundertvierzig

2. Card: 8 − 5 =    A. dreizehn
                    B. vier
                    C. drei

Correct responses: A, C

**5.7.4**  *Key-Word Comprehension*

Correct identification or completion of many comprehension items depends on a student's ability to isolate the key word (or words) in a rapidly spoken sentence or dialogue. According to the difficulty of the key word, an item is classified as a vocabulary item (difficult) or a comprehension-ease item (easy). In making this distinction, one assumes that if the item were read very slowly and distinctly, all students would correctly identify a comprehension-ease item, whereas only those who knew the difficult key words would identify vocabulary items correctly.

Comprehension items should be prepared in advance and later reviewed in order to eliminate ambiguities.

**5.7.4a** BRIEF DIALOGUE

You will hear a brief dialogue. Decide whether the last response is appropriate or inappropriate. Indicate your answer as follows: A = appropriate , B = inappropriate .

Here is a sample item in Italian:

— Dimmi, ti piace giocare al tennis?
— Mi piace, sì; ma preferisco giocare al baseball.

Correct response: A

**5.7.4b** SITUATION

You will hear a short dialogue followed by a descriptive statement. Choose the appropriate response.

Here is a sample item in German:

„Was möchten Sie?"
„Eine Bratwurst, bitte, und ein Glas Milch."
„Ein Moment, bitte."

Die Dame ist wahrscheinlich    A. im Bus.
    B. im Konzert.
    C. im Restaurant.

Correct response: C

**5.7.4c** QUESTION-ANSWER

You will hear a question followed by a series of answers. Select the most appropriate answer to the question and mark the corresponding space on your answer sheet.

Here is a sample item in German:

Wann essen Sie?    A. Um sechs.
    B. Auf der Straße.
    C. Mit meiner Familie.

Correct response: A

**5.7.4d** STATEMENT-REJOINDER

You will hear a sentence spoken; after a slight pause you will hear three (or four) additional sentences. From the three (or four) sentences select the one that would continue the conversation along the same lines.

Here is a sample item in German:

Ich studiere Geschichte.  A. Das möchte ich auch.
B. Ich kenne sie nicht.
C. Ich wasche mich auch.

Correct response: A

### 5.7.4e COMPLETION OF THOUGHT

You will hear a sentence followed by a series of sentences (or part of a sentence followed by a series of phrases). Select the sentence (or phrase) that most appropriately complements the stem (the original sentence or phrase).

Here is a sample item in English:

I would like to eat now.  A. I'm very hungry.
B. The movie sounds terrific.
C. Jimmy likes her, too.

Correct response: A

Here is a sample item in German:

Der Briefträger bringt uns  A. die Post.
B. die Haare.
C. kleine Kinder.

Correct response: A

For types 5.7.4b through 5.7.4e, the choices should all be of about the same length.

### 5.7.5 *False Cognates*

Words with similar forms in the native language and the target language but with different meanings present a particular learning problem. Items similar to those in Section 5.7.4 can be used to measure the student's ability to discriminate among these difficult words. In a test based on cognates, both true and false cognates should be included so that the student will not assume that all items appearing to be cognates are false ones and automatically discard them in his selection of responses.

Here is a sample item in French (item type 5.7.4e):

Mon frère ne pouvait pas finir ses devoirs de français hier soir, et alors

A. j'y assistais.
B. je l'ai attendu.
C. je l'ai aidé.

Correct response: C

In English this item would read: My brother couldn't finish his French homework last night, and so

A. I was there.
B. I waited for him.
C. I helped him.

### 5.7.6  *Passage Comprehension*

Passage comprehension may be used with intermediate and advanced students. Since the aim of such a test is to evaluate the student's ability to follow a long passage or conversation, the questions must be framed in an unambiguous and easily comprehensible format. In other words, a student should not do poorly on a passage-comprehension test because, although he did understand the passage, he was misled by the wording of the questions. If the problem lies in the phrasing of the question itself, then it is a waste of time to have the students listen to the passage.

Before the test the teacher should let the students know whether the passage will be read once or twice. Under no circumstances should the teacher reread certain sentences at the request of the students.

The following types of items may be employed to measure the students' degree of comprehension.

#### 5.7.6a  PURE TEST:[1] TRUE-FALSE

You will hear the passage once. Then you will hear a series of sentences, each read only once. Listen carefully to each sentence and determine whether, according to the passage, it is true or false. Indicate your answer as follows: A = | true |, B = | false |.

#### 5.7.6b  PURE TEST: QUESTION-ANSWER

You will hear the passage once. After the completion of the passage, you will hear a series of questions concerning the passage. Each question will be followed by three (or four) suggested responses, A, B, and C (and D). On your answer sheet, blacken the space corresponding to the appropriate response.

#### 5.7.6c  PURE TEST: DRAWING

You will hear the passage once. Then sketch rapidly the scene that has been described (or a map of the scene).

---

[1] On a *pure* test, the student uses only the one skill being evaluated. On a *hybrid* test, the student must use two or more skills.

**5.7.6d** HYBRID TEST: TRUE-FALSE

You will hear the passage once. Then turn to your answer booklet. You will see a series of statements referring to the passage. Decide whether each statement is true or false. Indicate your answer as follows: A = | true |, B = | false | .

**5.7.6e** HYBRID TEST: QUESTION-ANSWER
(oral questions and printed responses)

You will hear the passage once. Then turn to your answer booklet. You will hear a series of questions concerning the passage. Upon hearing the question, read the suggested responses in your answer booklet and indicate the appropriate one by marking the corresponding space on your answer sheet.

**5.7.6f** HYBRID TEST: QUESTION-ANSWER
(printed questions and responses)

You will hear the passage once. Then turn to your answer booklet. Read the questions and suggested responses in your answer booklet. Indicate your answers by blackening the corresponding spaces on your answer sheet.

**5.7.6g** HYBRID TEST: QUESTION-ANSWER
(printed questions and written responses)

You will hear the passage once. Then turn to your test booklet and answer the questions about the passage in French (the target language).

(The teacher should announce in advance whether the responses are to be judged just for content, or for both content and form.)

(If the teacher wishes to evaluate *only* listening comprehension, then the pure tests, Items 5.7.6a through 5.7.6c, yield the most valid results. Items 5.7.6d through 5.7.6f introduce the additional skill of reading. Item 5.7.6g requires both reading and writing. It should also be noted that by using oral questions (Items 5.7.6a, 5.7.6b, and 5.7.6e), the teacher can control the time spent on each item and be certain that all students finish the test at the same time.)

## 5.8 LISTENING COMPREHENSION: SYNTAX AND GRAMMAR

In order to understand the target language, the student must be able to recognize the patterns of that language. Although the ability to identify the syntax and the grammar of a language does not of itself imply the ability to use these elements in speaking, it is nonetheless true that unless the student can recognize patterns he will not be able to employ them with assurance and accuracy. In beginning classes it is essential that students hear the differences in the forms of the target language and that they understand the role played by different elements in the sentence.

Only items that are grammatically correct should be employed. Elementary and intermediate students should never be asked whether a certain sentence is correct or not; such items should only be used in teacher-preparation classes, and even in such instances, students profit most from continual confrontation with correct forms.

### 5.8.1 *Identification of Forms*

The teacher often wishes to determine whether the student can easily recognize specific grammatical forms of the target language. Such items may be incorporated into diagnostic quizzes; for, until all students can identify given forms, it is futile to engage in more complex discussions, explanations, or drills utilizing these forms. Brief quizzes incorporating the following item types may be given frequently in elementary classes. (These items differ from those given in Sections 5.3 and 5.4; here gross distinctions rather than minimal-pair differences are tested.)

#### 5.8.1a VERB TENSES

You will hear a series of short sentences. Listen carefully and decide whether the verb is present or imperfect. Indicate your answer as follows:

A = present , B = imperfect .

Here are some sample items in French:

1. Jean était ici.
2. Marie finissait sa leçon.
3. Vous finissez votre leçon.

Correct responses: B, B, A

The specific tenses and the key would be modified according to the specific material being covered.

#### 5.8.1b NUMBER

You will hear a series of short sentences. Decide whether the subject in each sentence is singular or plural. Indicate your answer as follows: A = singular , B = plural (if appropriate: C = either singular or plural ).

Here are some sample items in German:

1. Die Häuser sind grau.
2. Die Frau kommt gleich.
3. Unser Hund schläft.

Correct responses: B, A, A

The directions may be modified so that the student is asked to describe the direct object, the last word in the sentence, the noun (in sentences having only one), the pronoun, etc.

### 5.8.2 *Pattern Practice*

Most pattern practices can be used in simple listening tests. The specific directions, or model, will depend on the type of exercises composing the quiz.

#### 5.8.2a PATTERNS: SIMPLE VERSION

For each item you will hear two sentences. Listen carefully and decide whether the second sentence is in accordance with the first. Indicate your answer as follows: A = | appropriate | , B = | inappropriate | .

For example, here are some German sample items in which the direct object is to be replaced by the corresponding pronoun:

1. Ich sehe den Hund. Ich sehe ihn.
2. Ich kenne den Mann. Ich kenne sie.
3. Er kauft das Bild. Er kauft es.

Correct responses: A, B, A

#### 5.8.2b PATTERNS: MULTIPLE VERSION

(Specific directions describe the type of pattern to be followed.)

You will hear the key sentence read once. Then you will hear three (or four) responses. Indicate on your answer sheet the response that corresponds to the key sentence.

Here is a sample item in German similar to Item 5.8.2a.1 above:

Ich sehe den Hund.   A. Ich sehe ihn.
                     B. Ich sehe sie.
                     C. Ich sehe es.

Correct response: A

### 5.8.3   *Syntax and Structure: Pictures*

One of the most troublesome areas in which the target language differs from the students' native language is syntax. German, for example, primarily indicates the relationship between parts of the sentence through the use of inflected endings; English generally uses word order. Picture items can be developed to test whether the student understands the syntax and structure of the target language. However, these should first be tried out on another teacher, since pictures can often be interpreted in various ways.

> You will hear two sentences for each picture. Indicate which sentence describes the picture most accurately.

Here is a sample item in French:

A. Marie court vite mais Georges court plus vite qu'elle.

B. Marie court vite mais Georges court moins vite qu'elle.

Correct response: A

Here is a sample item in German:

A. Der Mutter gibt das Kind das Buch.
B. Die Mutter gibt dem Kind das Buch.

Correct response: A

## 5.9   LISTENING COMPREHENSION: DIFFERENT TYPES OF SPEECH

Advanced students, familiar with the vocabulary and structure of the language, often find that they can understand the target language when it is enunciated clearly and distinctly but are less sure of themselves when colloquial expressions are used or when the language is spoken quickly or in a stylized manner.

### 5.9.1   *Formal Speech*

Advanced students generally do not find it too difficult to adapt to the measured delivery of a formal speech or lecture, but certain rhetorical conventions or unfamiliar constructions can present problems. The best way to evaluate the students' ability to understand formal language is through the use of a recording of a speech or lecture. Comprehension may be assessed in the following ways.

### 5.9.1a  QUESTIONS

Item types 5.7.6a through 5.7.6g may be adapted for use here. To shorten the required retention span, the tape may be stopped at intervals and questions asked on the preceding portion. Another possibility is to allow the student to make notes which he may consult in answering the questions.

### 5.9.1b  NOTES

More advanced students may be asked to take notes in outline form. Such a test is no longer a pure listening test, but one that evaluates the student's note-taking and organizational ability as well as his command of the written language.

The notes may be assigned three grades: comprehension (content), organization, and correctness (spelling and structure).

### 5.9.2  *Newscasts*

Radio and television newscasters are often very difficult to understand because of their stylized delivery. The teacher could obtain a recording of a live newscast. Student comprehension would be measured as in Section 5.9.1.

### 5.9.3  *Rapid Conversation*

Often the advanced student who was able to get along satisfactorily in the target language in school is disappointed when traveling abroad by his inability to understand rapid conversation. If the teacher is able to obtain recordings of conversations between native speakers, these may be used in the classroom.

A recorded conversation may become the basis for a test using the items described above. To reinforce the correct responses and to verify the student's comprehension of more measured speech, the same conversation could be replayed a second time but with the participants enunciating more distinctly; the same questions could be asked twice and the results compared.

# CHAPTER SIX
# THE SPEAKING TEST

Recently foreign-language programs—from elementary school through college—have been gaining widespread support from parents eager to have their children learn to speak another language. Behind the development of new curricula and instructional materials and the construction of language laboratories throughout the country is a single aim: teaching the student to speak the language.

Yet all too frequently the speaking skill is more or less ignored when tests are being planned. While many teachers claim that they can assign overall grades for speaking ability according to class performance, such scores are to a certain extent subjective. In addition, if all formal tests are of the pencil-and-paper variety, students will quickly realize that their preparation is most profitably spent on reading and writing. The acquisition of fluent speech habits is relegated to the status of a pleasant luxury; students no longer consider it an essential goal of the course. An oral production test at the end of the term or semester will affirm the importance of the speaking skill.

Some students may be timid and even nervous about speaking tests. Others who read and write with difficulty can speak with confidence. For

**79**

these reasons speaking tests are sometimes termed "unfair." Yet if the speaking skill is to be learned, there must be a testing program.

## 6.1 GENERAL CONSIDERATIONS

Speaking is a social skill. Whereas one can read and write in private or listen to the radio or watch television alone, a person rarely speaks without an audience of some sort. Communication being the goal of the audio-lingual language program, emphasis is placed on the development of correct speech habits.

Even for those students who intend only to read the language, the acquisition of near-native pronunciation and intonation in the early stages of language learning provides a useful foundation. Many persons subconsciously use their speech muscles and vocal cords when reading, even though their lips do not move. Thus indirectly the time spent on reading a foreign language reinforces the student's speech habits.

Speaking, however, is more than pronunciation and intonation. At the functional level, speaking is making oneself understood. At a more refined level, speaking requires the correct and idiomatic use of the target language. The newcomer in a foreign country learns to express himself in order to obtain the essentials of life; first he uses gestures, then gradually he picks up words and phrases. But with no formal training and without the incentive for perfection, he retains a marked accent and uses simplified, and often inaccurate, structures.

In the classroom the language student is expected to learn correct pronunciation and speech patterns. The classroom setup usually offers less incentive for communication than the true-life situation; nevertheless, when communication is a class objective, the testing program should measure not only accurate expression but also ease and fluency in communication.

### 6.1.1 *Development of Speaking Tests*

In 1929, the Modern Foreign Language Study report on achievement tests pessimistically noted the impossibility of developing tests of oral proficiency that could be widely administered and that would yield results with any semblance of objectivity and comparability. However, four years later experiments were in progress using phonographic aluminum discs. In recent years the rapid growth of language laboratories has facilitated the administration of identical speaking tests to large groups of students. Trained scorers, often working in groups, have demonstrated the feasibility of rating student performance objectively. Only specific aspects of each utterance are scored, but the student does not know what the examiner will listen for. As early as the middle 1930's it was found that reliable scores could be obtained. This was confirmed by the Northeast Conference on the Teaching of Foreign Languages in the middle 1950's and then by the MLA Cooperative Foreign Language Tests, the MLA Proficiency Tests for Teachers and Advanced Students, and by a large-scale experiment conducted at the University of Colorado during 1960–62.

Unfortunately most speaking tests are tedious to score because each student tape contains the spoken cue as well as the student response, requiring the scorers to spend time listening to the same cues on every student tape. However, most new language-laboratory consoles have a switch that permits the teacher to activate student tapes so that only the response is recorded; in this way, scoring time is reduced by half.

### 6.1.2 *The Administration of Classroom Speaking Tests*

In the classroom the teacher will not be able to duplicate the rigorous conditions of standardized speaking tests in which each student records his own responses. Moreover, many schools do not have laboratories in which all students can be accommodated at "record" positions. Even if the speaking test can be administered in the laboratory, the teacher often discovers during the scoring that some tape recorders recorded poorly or not at all. Thus, some students must be called back for a second testing. Furthermore, listening to student tapes is a time-consuming task. Not only must the actual playing time be taken into account, but also the time needed to rewind the tape, take it off the machine, and thread the next tape. Cartridges can be manipulated more rapidly. If tapes are used, however, it is sometimes possible to have a student assistant duplicate all the student tapes on one long tape which the teacher must thread only once.

How can the busy teacher best evaluate student proficiency in speaking? Fortunately it has been found that formal speaking tests need not be given often: once a semester will suffice in high-school and college classes. Moreover, if the items are carefully chosen, the test itself can be quite short; much can be said in five minutes, much even in three. For this formal test the teacher can schedule each student individually.

During the year the teacher may give frequent informal speaking tests. The recitation of dialogues or the performance of pattern drills, for example, may be evaluated. Here, too, the teacher should prepare a scoring system so that every student is graded on specific aspects of his speech. In the elementary schools, such informal testing is very effective.

If the teacher monitors his students' work in the language laboratory, grades may be assigned regularly. Since the teacher will be tuning in on each student only for a few random responses during the period, he must use a global scoring system.[1]

This is a variation of the system suggested by Edward Stack in *The Language Laboratory and Modern Language Testing*.[2]

0 very poor response, no response
2 average response, neither excellent nor poor
5 superior response

Only the near-native response given immediately rates as 5; poor performance is given a 0. If the teacher knows that the performance is neither poor nor excellent, the student receives a 2; if the teacher hesitates in assigning the grade, a 2 is indicated. Over the semester the average of the student's scores will afford a fairly reliable gross estimate of his performance in the laboratory. A more refined evaluation of speaking proficiency, however, can only be obtained through a carefully structured speaking test.

## 6.2 OBJECTIVITY IN SPEAKING TESTS

Poorly planned speaking tests are usually unreliable instruments for assessing student proficiency. When using them, different teachers may assign different scores to the same utterance, and an individual teacher who hears the same utterance on two different occasions may not give it the same score each time.

### 6.2.1 *Scorer Reliability*

Scorer reliability is increased when judges evaluate only one aspect of the utterance, such as fluency,[3] overall intonation, or the production of a specific vowel or consonant. A numerical score is assigned to each utterance.

Consistency in scoring is of greater importance than the choice of a particular scoring system. Among the following possible breakdowns, each teacher should find one system that reflects his own scoring tendencies.

---

[1] In a global scoring system, the total sentence is evaluated. Such scores are much less reliable than those derived from the evaluation of one or two specific aspects of the sentence.

[2] Rev. ed. (New York: Oxford University Press, 1966), pp. 184–90. Stack gives a conversion table that makes it possible to record laboratory performance daily as a percentage grade.

[3] *Fluency* refers to both the rapidity of the response and the ease of delivery. Although fluency is a rather subjective quality, the individual teacher will be able to establish certain personal standards by which to judge the performances of his students. Scorer reliability is a function of the consistency with which these standards are applied.

### 6.2.1a  ONE CATEGORY

This simplified method works well with specific features of pronunciation
—such as proper intonation or an appropriately stressed syllable—where
there are no gradations of correctness.

0  wrong
1  right

### 6.2.1b  THREE CATEGORIES

0  no response; partial incomprehensible response
1  poor: total response but unacceptable results
2  acceptable: comprehensible in spite of minor errors
3  fluent

### 6.2.1c  FOUR CATEGORIES

0  no response; partial incomprehensible response
1  poor: total response but unacceptable results
2  fair but with definite faults
3  good but not quite perfect
4  perfect performance

### 6.2.1d  FIVE CATEGORIES

0  no response; partial incomprehensible response
1  poor: total effort but incomprehensible response
2  fair: faulty production but more or less comprehensible
3  acceptable: comprehensible but with minor faults
4  excellent: but short of perfect
5  superior: perfect performance

### 6.2.1e  MORE THAN FIVE CATEGORIES

Although it is possible to devise scales with six or more categories or to
establish a numerical continuum from 0 to 10, most people experience difficulty in maintaining a precise system of evaluation when they must select one
score from more than five choices. Scorer reliability tends to suffer.

If an item is to be weighted so that it numerically represents a possible 8
points, it is usually advisable to score on the more reliable four-category
scale and multiply the results by 2.

Sometimes student performance seems to fall between two given categories.
The teacher should determine in advance how such cases are to be handled.
One way would be to give the student the higher of the two marks the first
time a dubious situation arises, the lower mark the second time. The teacher
must, of course, be consistent in his application of this system.

### 6.2.2 *Using an Evaluation Sheet*

Since a scoring system for even the briefest speaking test must be determined in advance, the teacher will find that he can save time by also preparing some sort of evaluation sheet before administering the quiz or test.

#### 6.2.2a ROLL BOOK

For brief informal quizzes the class roll book may be used for entering the
scores. The columns are marked in advance according to the aspects of speech
production being tested. As each response is given, a number is entered in
the appropriate square. Totals and grades are determined after class. See the
sample page below.

| | /o/ (no glide) | /r/ (final position) | Fluency | Total |
|---|---|---|---|---|
| Billy Adams | | | | |
| | | | | |
| Susan Brown | | | | |
| | | | | |
| Joe Bruno | | | | |

FIG. 16

Each student may be asked three questions or may be instructed to read
or recite three lines; the teacher may call on students in random order to
maintain attention. The students are unaware of which aspects of speech
production are being evaluated. Different aspects would be assessed on
different days so that most of the important aspects would eventually be
evaluated.

#### 6.2.2b STANDARD ANSWER SHEET

For short tests containing a maximum of twenty sentences, the teacher
could adapt the answer sheet described in Section 2.2 and use it as an evaluation sheet. A four-category scoring system would be used, with A equal to
superior and D equal to poor; if no response is given, E is circled.

On a separate sheet of paper the teacher prepares the aspects to be scored. The items are so spaced that the answer sheet can be easily aligned with the corresponding descriptions. The student hears and responds to the twenty items in consecutive order. After all the tests have been administered, totals are determined and a general score given.

Here is a sample sheet and scoring system:

| 1. /a/ | 1. Ⓐ B C D E |
| 2. /1/ | 2. A B Ⓒ D E |
| 3. verb form | 3. A Ⓑ C D E |
| 4. quickness of response | 4. A B Ⓒ D E |

| 20. fluency | 20. A Ⓑ C D E | | | | |
|---|---|---|---|---|---|
| TOTALS | 6 | 7 | 5 | 1 | 1 |
| Multiply by | 4 | 3 | 3 | 1 | 0 |
| GRAND TOTAL | 24 +21 + 15 + 1 = 61 | | | | |

Fig. 17

In this test the maximum score is 80 (20 correct responses $\times$ 4).

### 6.2.2c SPECIAL FORM

For a semester or year-end final speaking test a special evaluation form may be devised that is appropriate to the test. Pronunciation items and the scoring indications for these items and for other sections of the test would be mimeographed so that a separate copy of the scoring sheet could be used for each student. Such a special form is especially useful in administering equivalent speaking tests to several different sections of the same course, whether taught by the same teacher or different teachers.

The following scoring sheet was designed for a first-year high-school French class:

---

French Speaking Test

Pupil's name_____

Part A:

 Notre neveu est plus jeune qu'Henri. C'est un enfant
       0 1    0 1   0 1 0 1
intelligent mais ses notes ne sont pas bonnes. Il ne
  0 1          0 1
travaille pas parce qu'il préfère passer son temps dans les
 0 1       0 1
montagnes.
 0 1

               Fluency: 0 1 2 3

Part B:

| | | | |
|---|---|---|---|
| J'ai acheté un ananas. | /a/ 0 1 | /e/ 0 1 | Fluency: 0 1 |
| Elle mange des sandwiches. | /ã/ 0 1 | /wiʃ/ 0 1 | Fluency: 0 1 |
| On le met dans le réfrigérateur. | /ə/ 0 1 | even stress, accent on last syllable: "réfrigérateur" 0 1 | Fluency: 0 1 |

Part C:

| | | | |
|---|---|---|---|
| Oui, je me baigne demain. | "me" 0 1 | "baigne" 0 1 | Fluency: 0 1 |
| Oui, je viens vous voir. | "viens" 0 1 | "vous" 0 1 | Fluency: 0 1 |
| Non, je n'ai pas aimé les fraises. | "ai...aimé" 0 1 | "n'... pas" 0 1 | Fluency: 0 1 |

           Total score:_____
        Total possible score: 30

Fig. 18

As the student reads the first paragraph (Part A) from his unmarked copy of the text, the teacher listens for the underlined sounds and liaisons. If the student produces the sound or makes the liaison correctly, 1 is circled. If his production is not perfect, 0 is circled. At the end of the text, the teacher quickly marks the student's fluency on a 0–3 scale (3 being perfect).

As the student answers the questions in Parts B and C, the teacher listens for certain sounds and structures and scores the student's performance 0 or 1. Later the circled numbers are added up and the total score is recorded.

## 6.3   ANALYZING THE PROBLEMS OF PRONUNCIATION AND INTONATION

If every phonemic feature of the target language were to be judged—scorer reliability requires that only one feature, or at most two, be evaluated per utterance—the comprehensive speaking test would attain unmanageable proportions. Fortunately a contrastive analysis of the sounds of English and of the foreign language under study will show that many phonemic features of the two languages are so similar that they pose little difficulty for the student. Consequently, the speaking test becomes "comprehensive" if the production of all the problem features, and only those, is evaluated.

Pronunciation and intonation problems may be traced to differences between the native language and the target language; thus, there are not simply problems for students of French, but, more precisely, certain problems for English-speaking students of French, others for Spanish-speaking students of French, etc. For most American foreign-language teachers the basic list of pronunciation problems will be limited to those encountered by English-speaking students. In certain parts of the United States, however, where there are students whose native tongue is not English, the teacher may discover other pronunciation problems. In sections of Florida, for example, French teachers might observe among Spanish-speaking students certain pronunciation problems arising from differences between French and Spanish.

What are the problem areas that must be tested? In Section 5.2, which described testing the skill of listening, two aspects of sound discrimination were discussed. Every student must learn to distinguish among the phonemes of the target language and to differentiate the distinctive phonetic features of the target language and his own. Unless the student can discriminate the sounds accurately, he can only hope to produce them in a haphazard fashion: his own ear must control his production. However, learning to identify the phonemes of a new language does not of itself imply the ability to produce those sounds, hence the need for sound-production tests to determine the quality of student pronunciation and intonation.

*All* the problems of sound discrimination that arise—for example, when English-speaking students are learning Spanish—must be incorporated into sound-production tests.

In addition to these areas of listening discrimination, the speaking tests must also include all cases where students tend to transfer English speech habits to the target language. One persistent habit that American students erroneously tend to transfer to Spanish, French, German, and other languages is the reduction of unstressed vowels. For most Americans, the following underlined vowels are all pronounced the same: "palatable," "benefit," "civilize," "phonograph," "suppression."

Another problem arises when the foreign language possesses only one vowel sound in instances where English has two or more sounds. For example, American students have little or no difficulty in distinguishing the sound /a/ in French or Spanish, because a similar phoneme exists in English. However, in speaking French or Spanish, American students frequently transfer other English pronunciations of the letter *a* to the target language, and the French *panne* or Spanish *pan* becomes not /pan/ but /pæn/.

More difficult are the cases in which similar phonemes exist in both languages but in different combinations. Linguists term this a problem of *distribution*. The English word "sank" has a nasal vowel, a consonant /ŋ/, and a final /k/ and is pronounced /sɛ̃ŋk/; the French *cinq* is similar but the /k/ immediately follows the vowel: /sɛ̃k/. The English student experiences great difficulty in trying to eliminate the consonant /ŋ/ from his production of the French word. In a more general sense, the fact that English nasal vowels are always followed by nasal consonants explains why so many students of French tend to nasalize vowels before *n* and *m*, contrary to French pronunciation habits, and to introduce an *n* or *m* between a nasal vowel and the following consonant.

The rhythm, stress, and intonation of the target language play an important role in communication. Too often teachers concentrate on perfecting the articulation of certain sounds while failing to establish the pattern of speech. Actually, the native Italian, for example, would find the speech of a student who used accurate rhythm and intonation but mispronounced several vowels or consonants much more acceptable than the speech of a student who made no errors in the individual sounds but spoke with a marked American rhythm and intonation. Each language has its characteristic pitch and intonation patterns for which the beginning student tends to substitute those of his native language.

In speaking Spanish, German, or other stressed languages, the student must also learn where to place the stress in each word; as is the case in English, the position of the stress often connotes meaning. In speaking French, the student experiences even more difficulty trying not to introduce a tonic and secondary stress in long words. Before developing pronunciation tests, the teacher should establish a list of the problems likely to be encountered by English-speaking students studying the target language.[1]

[1] Publications on this subject have been prepared under the auspices of the Center for Applied Linguistics: see Charles A. Ferguson, ed., Contrastive Structure Series. Also see Robert L. Politzer, *Teaching French*, 2nd ed. (New York: Blaisdell, 1965).

## 6.4 PRONUNCIATION TESTS

In the pronunciation items, the teacher will be evaluating the production of the segmental phonemes—vowels and consonants—of the target language. Since the pronunciation test should simulate the natural use of the language, the phonemes to be considered are incorporated into typical sentences.

To maintain the objectivity essential for arriving at a reliable score, the teacher should listen for only *one* aspect of each sentence or phrase. In order to take into consideration the fact that students will sometimes pronounce a sound correctly on one occasion and incorrectly on another, it is suggested that the key sound appear at least twice in the test items. Although the student obviously realizes that his speaking performance is being scored, he should not be aware which particular element is coming under the teacher's scrutiny. A variety of stimuli or cues may be employed to induce the student to utter the phrase or sentence desired.

### 6.4.1 *Mimicry*

The student is asked to repeat the sentence given as a model by the teacher. In a laboratory test, the cue could come from the console.

Bonjour Jeanne, comment ça va?   /a/

In the sentence above, the teacher would grade only the production of the phoneme /a/.

Très bien, merci, et toi?   /R/

Here the teacher listens only for the uvular *r*.

### 6.4.2 *Memorization*

The student recites from memory a poem or passage, or two students recite a dialogue. In order to grade each student's performance reliably, the teacher will have prepared a control version of the material as a scoring guide.

| | | |
|---|---|---|
| Les sanglots longs | 1. /e/ | no diphthong |
| Des violons | 2. /ɔ̃/ | as distinguished from /ã/; no *n*-sound |
| De l'automne | | after the vowel |
| Blessent mon cœur | 3. /l/ | no "dark" *l* |
| D'une langueur | 4. /œ/ | accuracy of production |
| Monotone. | 5. /ɔ/ | accuracy of production; no nasalization |
| | | on the third *o* |

Teachers finding it difficult to grade five features simultaneously would do well to concentrate on three sounds. Some may wish to reduce the scoring to three categories as follows (in such cases it is assumed that the key sound appears twice in the recitation):

1. both renditions poor
2. one good, one poor
3. both renditions good

In scoring a dialogue the teacher must establish parallel grading systems. Both students should be graded on the same sounds, even though these sounds will probably appear in a different sequence in the two parts of the dialogue.

### 6.4.3 *Oral Cue: Simple Patterns*

Pattern drills may be used as pronunciation tests. In order not to disadvantage the poorer students, these patterns should be very familiar. Since the teacher wishes to assess to what extent the student has mastered and assimilated the pronunciation features of the target language in his normal performance, it is preferable that such quizzes not be designated formal pronunciation tests.

Cue: Je rentre à midi.   (nous)
Response: Nous rentrons à midi.   /R/

### 6.4.4 *Oral Cue: Question and Answer*

Familiar questions and answers may also be employed as pronunciation tests.

Cue: Jean finit-il son travail?
Response: Oui, Jean (il) finit son travail.   /i/

(Both sounds should be identical. Avoid /ɪ/.)

### 6.4.5 *Oral Cue: Completion*

Well-worded completion items lead the student to pronounce a word that does not appear in the stem. Such an item eliminates simple imitation. Completion items must be carefully prepared in advance so that all students will furnish the desired word or phrase.

Cue: Man schneidet Fleisch mit einem . . .
Response: Messer   final   /ʌ/

### 6.4.6 *Reading: Familiar Material*

Once the reading skill has been introduced, written cues may be used to induce the student to pronounce words that have not previously been modeled. If the phrases are familiar, such a test will produce a fairly natural speech sample. Again the teacher should prepare for himself a special version of the text in which the elements to be scored are clearly indicated.

### 6.4.7 *Reading: New Material*

The pronunciation test based on new material not only measures the student's production of certain specific sounds but also indicates the accuracy and the rapidity with which he associates the sounds of the target language with the printed word. Many intermediate students, who have mastered the sounds of the new language, will perform unevenly on this type of test. Here, too, the teacher should carefully predetermine which sounds or combinations will be scored. Words that present the greatest difficulty are English cognates that are pronounced differently in the target language.

### 6.4.8 *Pictures*

Pronunciation tests with visual cues should not be confused with vocabulary tests. The former are most effectively used to bring the student to say a word that offers a particular pronunciation problem. It is often helpful to accompany the picture with a spoken or written cue.

Cue: Voilà des nombres entiers.   1, 2, 3
       Et voici des . . .      ½, ¼
Response: fractions

In this item the teacher should check /ksjɔ̃/; a common error is /kʃjɔ̃/.

## 6.5   INTONATION TESTS

Each language has its own intonation patterns, and often the dialects within a given language are in part characterized by their own intonation patterns. When learning a new language, the student tends to transfer the intonations of his native language to the target language. Cases in which this transfer can validly be made present no learning problem. In classroom testing the teacher need be principally concerned with two major types of intonation: those that distinguish the target language from the native language of the students and those that connote special meaning in the target language.

One major advantage of the dialogue-approach to language learning is that the student acquires an accurate conversational intonation from the beginning of his instruction. The flow of the phrase is introduced as an integral part of the language itself.

For intonation tests, items that permit the evaluation of one or two specific aspects of intonation should be prepared. First the teacher should have

at hand an outline of the general characteristics of the target-language intonation. He will also need a description of American English intonation patterns. By comparing these two outlines, he will discover the potential areas
of conflict, areas in which student performance should be tested.[1] During the
test he will grade the student's performance as acceptable or unacceptable on
each point.

### 6.5.1  *Mimicry*

The students repeat sentences after the teacher or after a model on tape.
Performance is graded as acceptable or unacceptable. Such tests are particularly useful with beginning students.

### 6.5.2  *Memorization*

In reciting memorized materials or dialogues previously studied in class or
in the laboratory, students generally use proper intonation. Performance is
graded as acceptable or unacceptable.

### 6.5.3  *Oral Cue*

A response is elicited either by a question or through a direction. Since the
student tends to concentrate on the content of his response, the teacher can
readily judge whether the intonation patterns of the target language have
become habits or whether the student reverts to the patterns of his native
language when under stress.

Here are two sample items in French:

Cue: Demandez à Pierre l'âge qu'il a.
Response: Quel âge avez-vous (as-tu) ?

Check whether the student continually employs a falling pitch.

Cue: Que feriez-vous si vous étiez riche?
Response: Si j'étais riche (1), j'irais en France (or some other appropriate
answer) (2).

Listen for a rising pitch at (1) and a falling pitch at the end of the sentence (2).

---

[1] See the Contrastive Structure Series, ed. Charles Ferguson (Chicago: University of
Chicago Press): William G. Moulton, *The Sounds of English and German* (1962),
chap. 11; Frederick B. Agard and Robert J. Di Pietro, *The Sounds of English and
Italian* (1965), chap. 6; Robert P. Stockwell and J. Donald Bowen, *The Sounds of
English and Spanish* (1965), chap. 3. See also Politzer, *Teaching French*, chap. 6.

### 6.5.4  *Visual Cue*

Students are asked to tell a story suggested by a series of drawings or to describe a picture. This type of test is less objective because different students will use different sentence structures. However, it is possible to evaluate the students' general intonation pattern on the following points:

1. intonation within word groups
2. intonation at the end of word groups
3. final intonation in declarative sentences

### 6.5.5  *Reading*

Each student is asked to read a passage aloud. This type of test may prove less satisfactory and less valid than the above types since reading intonation is often unnatural, even when students are requested to read aloud in their native language.

## 6.6  STRESS TESTS

Since most polysyllabic English words carry not only a primary stress, but also secondary and weak stresses, English-speaking students can usually hear and reproduce stress easily in other languages. English-speaking students do, however, face certain stress problems.

First, the American student tends to apply the English weak-stress pattern and the consequent vowel reduction to the target language. In a weak-stress position, most English vowels are pronounced identically, regardless of their spelling. Most English-speaking students must learn to overcome the tendency to reduce the unaccented or unstressed vowels of the target language.

Second, in a language with a stress system, special attention must be paid to cognates in which the positions of the stressed syllables do not correspond. For example, consider English *stúdent* and German *Studént*, or English *úniform* and Spanish *unifórme*. Often a misplaced stress will render the word incomprehensible to the native speaker of the language.

Third, in learning a language with no stress system, such as French, students must make a conscious effort not to introduce a primary stress inappropriately into long words.

Fourth, a different problem arises when the distribution of stressed syllables in the target language does not correspond with that in English. For example, the spondee, or succession of two stressed syllables, while rare in English, is frequent in Spanish. Students tend to introduce an inappropriate glottal stop [1] to separate the stressed syllables, for example, *habló alto*.

[1] The *glottal stop* is a consonant sound formed by a momentary closing of the vocal cords.

### 6.6.1 *Mimicry and Memorization*

Since most English-speaking students are conscious of stress, they tend to perform well on this type of test in languages such as German, Spanish, and Italian. In French, the items would be scored for absence of stress.

### 6.6.2 *Oral Cue with or without Picture*

For a stressed language, a question or completion-type item may be used to elicit the desired word. Often a picture or other visual cue is helpful. Such items should be constructed in advance and carefully reviewed in order to eliminate the possibility of ambiguity.

Here is a sample item in German:

Cue: Der Mann, der ein Flugzeug fliegt, ist ein . . .
Response: Pilot

In items of this type, the examiner is limited in his choice of vocabulary to words with which the student is actively familiar. Such items are consequently of limited usefulness. They fail to discriminate well between students who have acquired a feeling for the stress patterns of the target language and those who can mimic accurately but revert to English habits when faced with less familiar vocabulary.

### 6.6.3 *Reading*

A printed text to be read aloud affords the most reliable stress test. The teacher, uncritical of intonation or fluency, judges whether the students accentuate the proper syllables. Cognates not previously used in class may be included if their pronunciation reflects the regular patterns of the target language.

## 6.7 WRITTEN TESTS OF PRONUNCIATION, INTONATION, AND STRESS

There are certain written tests which are helpful in evaluating the students' knowledge of how the language is spoken. Such tests have two advantages: they can be scored rapidly, and they can be administered to the class as a group. English, because of its varied spellings, irregular stress patterns, and complex intonation, lends itself particularly well to this type of written testing.[1] The following written tests should be used sparingly, however, because students can learn pronunciation rules and still not pronounce well.

[1] See Robert Lado, *Language Testing* (New York: McGraw-Hill, 1964), pp. 95–104, 113–15, 137–39.

### 6.7.1 *Comparing Sounds*

For varied presentations of comparison items using three, four, and five options, see Section 5.2.

#### 6.7.1a SAME VS. DIFFERENT: TWO WORDS

Compare the underlined letters. If they represent the same sound, mark A; if they represent different sounds, mark B.

Here are two sample items in Spanish:

1. baso  vaso
2. duda

Correct responses: A, B

#### 6.7.1b SAME VS. DIFFERENT: THREE WORDS

Compare the sounds of the underlined letters. On your answer sheet indicate which two words contain underlined letters with the same sound.

Here are two sample items in French:

1. A. soi  B. sot  C. seau
2. Son chien (A) était bien (B) patient (C).

Correct responses: B, C; A, B

#### 6.7.1c RHYMES: TWO WORDS

Compare the two words and indicate whether they rhyme with each other; do not consider a "visual" rhyme, but only the sounds of the words. Mark A if they rhyme; mark B if they do not rhyme.

Here are two sample items in French:

1. ville, fille
2. faim, fin

Correct responses: B, A

#### 6.7.1d RHYMES: THREE WORDS

Compare the sounds of the three words. On your answer sheet indicate which two words of the group rhyme with each other.

Here are two sample items in German:

1. A. schöne  B. Söhne  C. rönne
2. A. den  B. wenn  C. zehn

Correct responses: A, B; A, C

Note: This technique of comparing sounds is effective with advanced students. When used for languages with fairly well-defined spelling systems, such items can measure the student's knowledge of the exceptions to the general patterns of pronunciation.

### 6.7.2   *Comparing Sounds: Omitted Letters*

In this type of item, the sounds to be compared are left blank. Consequently, the key word must be presented in an unambiguous context so that the problem of guessing does not interfere with student performance.

#### 6.7.2a   SIMPLE VERSION

On your answer sheet indicate in which words the omitted letters represent identical sounds.

Here is a sample item in French:

A. r__ponse   B. r__construction   C. r__connaître

Correct response: B, C

In some cases pictures may be included for the sake of clarity.

#### 6.7.2b   COMPLEX VERSION

On your answer sheet indicate which word or words contain underlined letters that sound the same as the letters omitted in the original sentence.

Here is a sample item in French:

Les Américains ont gagné leur indépend__ce.
A. pendent   B. bien   C. camp   D. panne

Correct response: C

### 6.7.3   *Locating Stress*

On your answer sheet indicate which syllable receives the greatest (primary) stress.

Here are some sample items in German:

1. A  B  C
   arbeitslos
2. A  B C D
   Toilettentisch
3. A  B  C D E
   Lockenperücke

Correct responses: A, B, A

### 6.7.4  *Comparing Stress*

On your answer sheet mark the letters of the two words which have the same stress pattern.

Here are two sample items in German:

1. A. Frühling   B. Bücher   C. Geschäft
2. A. heiraten   B. begreifen   C. rasieren

Correct responses: A, B; B, C

### 6.7.5  *Comparing Intonation*

Decide whether the intonation patterns of the two sentences are the same or different. On your answer sheet, indicate your answer as follows: A = same , B = different .

Here is a sample item in Spanish:

¿Tienes tiempo?      ¿De dónde viene?

Correct response: B

Intonation tests of this type present two drawbacks. First, it is difficult to formulate a sentence open to only one type of intonation. Second, students who are acquainted with the basic elements of intonation will often be able to select the correct response on paper even though they may lapse into English intonation patterns when speaking.

## 6.8  DIRECTED SPEAKING TESTS

Directed speaking tests measure the ease and accuracy with which the student handles the patterns of the target language. Since the range of correct responses is narrowly defined, the student's performance may be judged with high objectivity. Only the aspect under evaluation, that is, the use of structure and syntax, should be evaluated. Pronunciation enters into the judging only if it conveys the meaning of the response.

Generally speaking, most of the patterns drilled in class may be adapted with good results to the speaking test. The difference between the classroom drill and the informal test lies in the fact that no model is given in the latter. Instructions are given in English for beginning students and in the target language for more advanced students; it is essential that all students understand the directions.

### 6.8.1. *Multiple Substitution*

The student replaces one element in the sentence with another and is consequently obliged to effect other changes. Items are scored as either correct or incorrect for each required modification:

one changing element:    0  incorrect
                                         1  correct
two changing elements:    0  both incorrect
                                         1  one correct
                                         2  both correct
three changing elements:  0  all incorrect
                                         1  one correct
                                         2  two correct
                                         3  three correct

If desired, a second score could be given for fluency or promptness of response: 0 hesitating, 1 fluent. The response might receive a point for being fluent even though the changing elements were all incorrectly handled.

Here is a sample item in German that requires modification of the definite article:

Cue: Ich nehme das Buch.   (Bleistift)
Response: Ich nehme den Bleistift.

Similar items may be constructed to evaluate student proficiency in handling the indefinite and partitive articles; descriptive, demonstrative, and possessive adjective forms; pronouns, reflexives, verb forms, and sequence of tenses.

### 6.8.2 *Modified Substitution*

The student must modify the new element before substituting it in the key sentence.

Here is a sample item in Spanish:

Cue: Tengo un libro.   (ver)
Response: Veo un libro.

Similar items can be used to test noun forms, adjective forms, comparison of adjectives and adverbs, cardinal and ordinal numbers.

**6.8.3**   *Replacement*

The student replaces a noun or phrase with the appropriate pronoun.

Here is a sample item in French:

Cue: Les enfants vont à Nice.
Response: Ils vont à Nice.

Similar items can be used to evaluate student proficiency in handling personal, demonstrative, and possessive pronouns and the position of pronouns.

**6.8.4**   *Transformation*

The student changes a sentence according to precise instructions.

**6.8.4a**   NUMBER

Change the following sentence to the plural.

Here is a sample item in French:

Cue: Où est mon cheval?
Response: Où sont mes chevaux?

In this sentence there are three plural changes to be made by the speaker. In isolation or in combination the following elements can be used in this type of item: articles, adjectives, nouns, pronouns, verb forms. Changes may be made from singular to plural or from plural to singular.

**6.8.4b**   NEGATION

Change the following sentence to the negative.

Here is a sample item in German:

Cue: Ich habe es verkauft.
Response: Ich habe es nicht verkauft.

**6.8.4c**   INTERROGATIVE FORMS

Change the following statement into a question using the inverted form.

Here is a sample item in French:

Cue: Elle cherche son père.
Response: Cherche-t-elle son père?

**6.8.4d** VERB FORMS, MODES, AND TENSES

Convert the following sentence into the future.

Here is a sample item in Spanish:

Cue: El no trabaja.
Response: El no trabajará.

**6.8.5** *Following Commands*

This type of item parallels the classroom directed dialogue.

Here is a sample item in French:

Cue: Dites à Madame Lebrun de s'asseoir.
Response: Asseyez-vous, Madame.

Such items may be used to evaluate the student's command of first and second person verb forms in a variety of modes and tenses in addition to his mastery of pronoun forms and word order. It should be noted, however, that only the commands "ask" and "tell" reflect common use of the language.

The items would be scored on correctness of word order and of forms. Since such a test measures student command of the grammatical patterns of the language, comprehension problems should be avoided unless knowledge of difficult verb forms or noun forms is being tested.

**6.8.6** *Joining Sentences*

The student's ability to use conjunctions and relative pronouns, as well as his understanding of verb tenses, modes, and word order, may be evaluated with the following item type: given two independent statements, the student is asked to join them into one complex or compound sentence.

Here is a sample item in Spanish:

Cue: La casa es muy cómoda. Habitamos en la casa.
Response: La casa en que habitamos es muy cómoda.

**6.8.7** *Directed Questions and Answers*

In the question-answer speaking test, the student is told what kind of response to give. Although the student is not completely free to choose his answers in such a directed test, he often enjoys such items because they so closely approximate a real conversational situation.

Here is a sample item in French:

Cue: Croyez-vous qu'il sache chanter?   (oui)
Response: Oui, je crois qu'il sait chanter.

Note: In this particular example the student must modify two verb forms.

In a variation of this item type, the student is given the answer (perhaps on a sheet of paper) and asked to supply the appropriate question.

Here is a sample item in German:

Cue: Ich will das blaue Buch kaufen.
Response: Welches Buch wollen Sie (willst du) kaufen?

Such items may test verb forms, word order, the use of pronouns, and question words.

Questions may be asked about a picture or chart. If the speaking test is being held in the language laboratory, students may all be given a copy of the same picture, or a large picture may be placed within everyone's view. All students would be asked the same question simultaneously. Such a version of the question-answer test is particularly useful in testing active speaking vocabulary.

It should be noted that when pictures are used in a test, the teacher may soon discover that not every picture is appropriate. A picture often conveys very different messages to different observers. Only by experimentation can the teacher discover whether a particular picture is reasonably constant in the message it bears. Of course, in the classroom certain pictures or stick figures may have been incorporated into the instruction; these visual materials can be expected to elicit the desired responses.

### 6.8.8 *Numbers*

Ease in handling numbers may be tested orally, usually by means of a straight question-answer technique.

Here is a sample item in German:

Cue: Wieviel ist fünf und acht?
Response: Fünf und acht ist dreizehn.

If flash cards are used, the calculation to be performed is presented in figures and the student describes the calculation and the answer in the target language (the response would be similar to the sample above).

If props are available in the classroom for creating a commercial situation, a numbers test may be improvised. The simulated conversations may take place in a railroad station, in a restaurant, or in a store. A chart could be prepared beforehand clearly indicating specific fares or prices.

### 6.8.9 *Telling Time*

#### 6.8.9a CLOCK

With the aid of a large clock with movable hands, the teacher may ask each student to give the time orally.

#### 6.8.9b TIMETABLE

If a large timetable is available (or a regular timetable enlarged with an opaque projector), questions may be asked that concern arrivals and departures of trains or planes, the length of trips, the length of stops in various cities on the route, etc.

### 6.8.10 *Statement and Rejoinder*

In a statement-rejoinder item, the teacher speaks a sentence and then indicates by a gesture or a facial expression the type of reaction the student is to manifest. Not only the choice of the rejoinder, but also the promptness of the response and the appropriateness of the intonation may be scored. This type of informal classroom test affords the more creative students an opportunity to show their inventiveness and thus encourages the other students to listen to the answers.

Here is a sample item in French:

> Cue: Je ne peux pas venir.   (sad reaction)
> Response: Ah! quel dommage!

### 6.8.11 *Directed Conversation*

Two or more students are assigned roles and are given precise directions as to the type of conversation they are to engage in. For elementary classes the directions are best given in the target language, but for more advanced students they may be given in English if the teacher wishes to test fluency of vocabulary and structure. This test should not become an exercise in oral translation; that is, it should not be so difficult that the student must stop and grope for words. Sample directions could be given as follows:

> You are hungry and go into a restaurant. You wish to order ham and eggs and a glass of milk, but the waiter suggests steak, French fries, and a glass of wine. You agree to the steak and French fries but tell him you dislike wine. He suggests a glass of lemonade and you agree.

Such speaking tests should be scored primarily on choice of vocabulary, use of structures, and fluency of delivery. As we have mentioned, pronunciation is better tested separately.

### 6.8.12 *Oral Translation (Lightning Translation)*

Oral translation, done without the aid of a dictionary, may be employed with equal success, particularly with older students, in classes using the traditional or the modified audio-lingual approach. Many textbooks present a dialogue in the target language and, on a separate page, equivalent English forms. These English forms can provide the text for oral translation quizzes at the elementary level.

The English sentence is spoken once rapidly and the student gives the target-language equivalent as quickly and as fluently as possible. Since the emphasis is on equivalent structures, the intermediate student may be given some leeway in expression. Dialogue sentences can be modified in order to evaluate the student's ability to use structures in a variety of ways.

The student responses should be scored for their rapidity and fluency as well as their accuracy. If responses are sluggish and unnatural, such tests should be postponed or else simplified to cover only known dialogue.

### 6.8.13 *Picture Writing*

Thanks to a system of picture writing developed by TAVOR Aids,[1] it is possible to bypass both the native language and the skills of listening and reading in the target language and still elicit specific spoken responses. Whole ideas are represented through simple line drawings called "ideograms." Obviously the students will have to be familiar with the symbols before taking the test; however, this picture-writing technique will be a welcome addition to classroom teaching aids.

In an informal testing situation, the ideograms may be drawn on flash cards; for a formal test, mimeographed copies of the selected ideograms can be distributed.

Let us look at some examples in English.

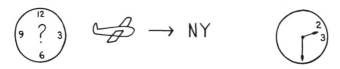

(When is there a plane for New York? *or* When does the plane leave for New York?)

Response: There is one at two-thirty. *or* At two-thirty.

[1] Interested teachers may request that their names be placed on the mailing list of *TAVOR Aids Bulletin*, which is distributed free of charge by TAVOR Aids, P.O. Box 282, Forest Hills, N.Y. 11375.

(What is the man planning to do?)

Response: He is going to the bookstore to buy a book. (The balloon contains symbols of the man's intentions. The symbol ⌃ represents a roof: thus, ⌂ is a bookstore. Similarly, ⊥ is a church, ⌂ is a butcher shop, etc.)

Another version:

Response: He is going to hold up the bookstore.[1]

## 6.9   FREE RESPONSE TESTS

The purest type of speaking test is the free response test. The student is free to talk about whatever he wishes for a stated period of time; usually one or two minutes is sufficient for beginning students. Although no thorough studies have been carried out to determine what effects preparation has on performance, it is customary to allow each student a minute or two to prepare his response.

### 6.9.1   *Pictures*

The teacher can provide a picture or series of pictures so that even those students who suddenly can think of nothing to say on a speaking test will have before them a subject for conversation. The student may describe the objects or the action taking place in the picture; he might tell a story merely suggested by the pictorial aid.

When such a test is administered in the language laboratory, all students are shown the picture, given the instructions, and allowed one minute to

[1] For similar ideograms, see *TAVOR Aids Bulletin*, No. 2 (February 1966), pp. 2–3.

plan what they will say. At a pre-arranged signal, all student tapes are activated and the students talk freely until a second signal is given and the tapes are stopped.

Such a test may be scored on vocabulary, structure, and fluency. Pronunciation and intonation may also be considered. In a two-minute test, however, it is preferable to score only two or three aspects of the student's performance.

### 6.9.2  *Conversation*

The most credible, or natural, type of speaking test is a free conversation with the teacher or with another qualified speaker. In the latter case, it is better to have the speaker talk with each student for several minutes. The teacher should try to remain as unobtrusive as possible, perhaps seated behind the student. While the speaker encourages the student to express himself, the teacher is free to concentrate on scoring the student's performance objectively.

Two teachers might help each other in such a testing session. Generally, it is better to have the visiting teacher speak with the students; this way the host teacher does not feel that his own performance is being judged by another. It is also possible to have an advanced student from another class, one who speaks the language easily and is able to put other students at ease, help with the testing session.

Before administering a conversation test, the teacher should plan a series of questions demanding more than perfunctory yes-no answers. Often a good starting question is one that asks the student what he would do if he had the money, the time, the opportunity, and so on. Such a question allows the student to orient the conversation. The teacher may then easily follow his response with queries like "Why?" or "Have you considered a different possibility?" "Which one?" "Why did you reject that idea?" etc. The questioner should realize that his primary functions are putting the student at ease, encouraging him to speak, and helping him out when necessary.

Such a test may be scored on fluency, ease of expression, accuracy of structure, intonation, and choice of vocabulary. The number of aspects to be scored depends on the length of the conversation, but these elements should be evaluated in the same order for each student. For example, as the student feels more at ease, he tends to become more fluent; fluency, then, might well be judged as the final aspect of the performance.

## 6.10   THE COMPREHENSIVE SPEAKING TEST

At the end of the semester, and often at mid-term, it is customary to have a fairly long examination. If one of the announced objectives of the course is speaking, then a speaking test should be considered part of the mid-term or final. If one-fourth of the emphasis of the course was devoted to the develop-ment of the skill of speaking, then one-fourth of the final exam grade should depend on the speaking test.

Since the speaking test is designed to evaluate individual performance, it must be administered to the students one by one, or to a group in the lan-guage laboratory if recording equipment is available. Generally the speaking test is given prior to the rest of the test, but all students should be told that their speaking performance constitutes a part of the final examination.

The comprehensive speaking test is composed of several sections in which the various aspects of the speaking skill are evaluated. If desired, written-answer speaking test items (as described in Section 6.7) may be included in the written section of the examination.

Here is a sample outline of the sections in a semester final:

| | |
|---|---|
| written test of pronunciation and stress: | 20% |
| pronunciation items: | 20% |
| directed responses: | 40% |
| free response: | 20% |
| | 100% |

Here is a sample breakdown of the items and time limits used in the test:

| | | |
|---|---|---|
| written test: | 20 | multiple-choice items. |
| pronunciation test: | 10 | mimicry sentences |
| | 5 | sentences to be read aloud |
| directed responses: | 20 | items |
| free response: | 2 | minutes |

A detailed answer sheet should be prepared to facilitate scoring. Some teachers prefer mimeographing these sheets so that one may be used for each student. If the test is to be administered in the language laboratory, the oral cues must be recorded in advance. Also, enough copies of the sentences to be read aloud must be mimeographed so that each student will have one in his booth. Any picture to be used for the free response section must also be selected in advance.[1]

If the language laboratory does not contain sufficient recording equip-ment, the teacher will have to arrange individual appointments with the stu-dents. In such a case, each student must receive equivalent but different items to reduce the possibility of test leakage. Several alternate sentences or items are prepared for each part of the examination; in large multisection courses, as many as ten alternates per item can be composed but each alternate is scored

---

[1] For a description of German comprehensive speaking tests and scoring sheets, see George A. C. Scherer and Michael Wertheimer, *A Psycholinguistic Experiment in Foreign-Language Teaching* (New York: McGraw-Hill, 1964), pp. 117–28.

for precisely the same features. For the free response section, several pictures should be available.

When individual speaking tests take place, the teacher is usually more at ease in scoring student performance if another qualified speaker—perhaps an advanced student—gives the oral cues. If possible, the speaking test should provide a satisfying experience for the student and permit him to demonstrate his newly acquired or growing skill in conversing in the target language.

# CHAPTER SEVEN

# THE READING TEST

Reading used to be the principal aim of most foreign-language courses. Since the study of literature, which for centuries represented the educational goal of the elite, requires only a reading knowledge of foreign languages, the terms "language" and "literature" were formally equated in the curriculum. The skill of reading, given priority over other language skills, was developed and evaluated through textual analyses, vocabulary tests, and translations into English; listening and speaking were merely the by-products of reading. In Europe, where such a system is still widely used, the student, to supplement his classroom training in reading and writing, may spend several summers in some foreign country to develop his fluency in speaking and listening. In the United States during the 1930's, the Modern Language Association proposed that the primary aim in teaching a foreign language was to enable students to read foreign texts in the original. This is the rationale behind the Ph.D. language requirement that a doctoral candidate prove his ability to read the literature in his specialty in two foreign languages. This reading knowledge is generally tested by a translation of a scholarly text into English.

The audio-lingual approach to instruction, which blossomed after World War II and received great impetus at the time of the Russian launching of Sputnik, places the emphasis elsewhere. Language, insist the New Key proponents, is *spoken* first; the written form frequently is but a transcription of an audio-lingual phenomenon. As for Ph.D. requirements, most linguists will not deny that with a rudimentary grammar book, a good dictionary, and some imagination a candidate will be able to pass the "reading" translation test, but, they add, this experience is not one of reading but of decoding or deciphering. When the student is learning to *read* a foreign language, his mind should be functioning in that language. To implement this, new words, particularly at the elementary level, should be introduced at widely spaced intervals, and they should be accompanied, if possible, with definitions or glosses in the target language. Today there is a new goal in reading—not verbatim translation but total comprehension without recourse to English.

## 7.1 GENERAL CONSIDERATIONS

Reading, by definition a language skill, requires a familiarity on the part of the reader with the two fundamental building blocks of the particular language under study: structure and vocabulary. The broader the student's knowledge of structure and the greater his vocabulary—regardless of how these two were acquired—the more difficult the texts he will be able to approach.

Of the two building blocks, structure is the more important. A student can usually find the meanings of new words in a dictionary, but unless he understands the relationships between the words, unless he is certain of structure, he will be unable to read the text accurately and to understand what he is reading. Consequently, two general types of test items are necessary to evaluate student reading potential: vocabulary items and structural (syntactical and morphological) items.

Furthermore the reading skill involves special features that distinguish it from the other language skills. First, reading requires visual perception (except for the blind, who depend on tactile recognition). Just as the young child must first be able to recognize the alphabet of his native language when learning to read, so must the student of a second language become familiar with the characters of that language. The alphabets of French, Spanish, and Italian present little difficulty to the literate American; German texts are now generally printed in familiar Roman type. American students *do* require pre-reading instruction in certain languages—Russian, Greek, Arabic, Hebrew, and Chinese, for example.

Reading can be differentiated from writing, speaking, and listening by another characteristic: speed. In learning a new language the student wishes eventually to read it easily and rapidly. Fluency in speaking and ease in listening comprehension correspond to speed in reading.

Familiarity with structure, a solid passive vocabulary, accurate visual perception, and speed all play their roles in reading comprehension; but it should be remembered that not all students attain equal proficiency in reading comprehension even in their native language. Since reading-comprehension items in the foreign language are constructed around whole sentences, or, more frequently, entire paragraphs or passages, student differences in verbal ability must be taken into consideration.

## 7.2   PRE-READING TESTS

If listening and speaking have been taught for a period of time before the presentation of reading and writing, then the pre-reading experience will entail the linking of known sounds to written symbols. This experience resembles to some extent the way in which young children learn to read their native language. Similarly, if the characters of the new language are unfamiliar, they, too, must be mastered during a period of pre-reading instruction. For a language with non-Roman characters, such as Russian, or with non-Roman characters and a direction of writing different from English, such as Hebrew or Arabic, the pre-reading period requires a great deal of effort on the part of the student. Classroom quizzes often help break the inevitable monotony of instruction.

### 7.2.1   *Identification*

Anyone who has learned to read English has developed a sensitivity to seemingly slight differences among printed letters—the difference between *e* and *c* for example. In learning to read a language with a non-Roman alphabet, students must become so familiar with the new alphabet that the identification of letters becomes automatic. In learning non-European languages where single characters represent syllables or whole words, students face a more difficult problem of identification. Facility in handling the new characters can be evaluated by measuring the speed at which the student can identify the characters. Quizzes like those suggested below should contain a substantial number of items. When the first student to reach the end of the quiz raises his hand, the others are told to stop working. Some teachers may give the test a fixed time limit. In either case, the student's score is based on the number of correct items; the time allowed for the test may also be indicated so that students can evaluate their improvement.

**7.2.1a** LETTERS

Circle the letter (character) that is the same as the first letter (character).

Here is a sample item in Russian:

Ж    Ш  Щ  Ж  Ч  Д

**7.2.1b** WORDS OR SENTENCES

Indicate which word (or sentence) is the same as the first word (or sentence).

Here are sample items in Russian:

1. НО′СИМ          A.  НО′СИТ
                   B.  НО′СИМ
                   C.  НО′СИТЕ
                   D.  НО′СЩЬ

2. ВИ′ДЯТ          A.  ВИ′ДИТ
                   B.  ВИ′ДИМ
                   C.  ВИ′ДИТЕ
                   D.  ВИ′ДЯТ

Correct responses: B, D

Note: This type of item may be rendered more difficult by writing the options across the page.

3. СТОЮ́     A.  СТОЯ́Т        B.  СТО́ЙТЕ

            C.  СТО́ЙТ         D.  СТОЮ́

Correct response: D

## 7.2.2  *Pictures to Words*

One elementary pre-reading test requires the identification of the printed word corresponding to a familiar picture. Here, although the student must be familiar with the word indicated by the picture, he must not necessarily be acquainted with the incorrect choices. If the language being studied has a spelling system that corresponds closely to the spoken word (as is the case with German and Spanish), such a test will be relatively easy. With French, where the "fit" between the spoken language and written language is not as tight, the items are more difficult.

Here is a sample item in Spanish:

        A.  casa
        B.  caso
        C.  causa

Correct response: A

### 7.2.3  *Spoken to Printed Words*

If speaking has been taught before reading, the teacher will want to measure the facility with which students can link the spoken word to its written form. Although this type of pre-reading test (or quiz, since such items are generally used in brief informal tests) resembles many commercial standardized listening-discrimination tests in which the student is asked to match an oral stimulus with the proper printed option, the two tests differ in use and function. The hybrid listening-discrimination test with a printed answer sheet is valid for students whose knowledge of the written language is distinctly superior to their listening ability: it is assumed that the students have no difficulty in linking sounds to spelling and that the crucial factor determining their choice of responses is the power to retain and discriminate among sounds.

The pre-reading test, in which spoken stimuli are matched with printed responses, may be used in two ways: in teaching the graphic forms of languages employing a non-Roman alphabet and in testing spelling ability (as a passive function) in languages with a Roman alphabet. Regarding the former case, it may be pointed out that some colleges offer courses in spoken Chinese and spoken Arabic; writing is not introduced until several semesters later. By that time the teacher will have had many opportunities to verify the students' ability in listening discrimination. When work in writing and reading is begun, the problem for these students will be to establish the relationship between spoken word and printed form.

Students learning languages that do employ the Roman alphabet will need a much shorter introduction to listening and speaking before coming into contact with the printed language. In the pre-reading test in such languages, only familiar words or phrases are read, or, for older students, words similar to known vocabulary and regular in spelling.

#### 7.2.3a  THREE PRINTED OPTIONS

Indicate which word on your answer sheet corresponds to the word you hear.

Here is a sample item in Spanish:

  (on tape): cuento    A.  cuento
                       B.  ciento
                       C.  quedo

THE READING TEST **113**

Correct response: A

The voice on the tape could speak short phrases or sentences.

Here is a sample item in French:

(on tape) : nous savons     A. nous avons
                                 B. nous savons
                                 C. nos savons

Correct response: B

**7.2.3b** THREE (FOUR) ORAL OPTIONS

You will hear three (four) words spoken. Indicate which one corresponds to the word on your answer sheet.

Here is a sample item in Italian:

(on tape) : A. Eccoli!      1. Eccoli!     A   B   C   (D)
              B. Eccola!
              C. Eccole!
           (D. Eccolo!)

Correct response: A

Short phrases or sentences may also be used in this type of item.

## 7.3   DISCRETE READING-COMPREHENSION ITEMS

In audio-lingual classes, beginning students learn to read only sentences and passages containing patterns that they can already handle orally. Multiple-choice items allow the teacher to measure the students' reading skill independently of their writing ability. Such items use words and patterns that the student already knows, but the items are original because they combine familiar material in new ways.

If the resulting items, especially in the early stages of language learning, appear too easy, they may be administered in a speed test. Two procedures are possible. In the first, sufficient time is allowed to enable all students to complete the quiz, but those who finish before the time limit are told to turn over their papers, note the time, and quietly read or do written exercises at their seats. Younger students may be asked to raise their hands when they have finished. In the second, the teacher announces in advance the amount of time allotted, and all students stop together when the time has expired.

### 7.3.1   *True-False Items*

Students are asked to read a series of statements and mark them as true (T) or false (F). (Later, in a written exercise, the students may be asked to revise the incorrect statements.)

Here are two sample items in French:

La neige est blanche.   (T)
Jacques est ma sœur.   (F)

### 7.3.2   *Appropriate-Inappropriate Items*

A large picture or poster is displayed to the class or a print is shown by an opaque projector. Each student is given a list of sentences to read. If a sentence is appropriate to the picture, the student marks plus $(+)$; if the sentence is inappropriate, he marks minus $(-)$. (In a written exercise, the students may be asked to correct the inappropriate statements.)

### 7.3.3   *Completion Items*

The student reads the first part of a sentence and then chooses which word(s) or phrase finishes the sentence most appropriately. Various aspects of the target language may be tested in this way.

#### 7.3.3a   VOCABULARY

Completion items may be constructed in which the selection of the correct response hinges on a knowledge of vocabulary.

Here are two sample items in French:

1. Je voudrais boire     A. des prières.
                         B. du lait.
                         C. des poires.

Correct response: B

This item is intended to check familiarity with the word *boire*. The distractor *prières* was chosen for its resemblance to the word *bière*. *Poires* is similar in spelling to *boire*. If *lait* is not familiar enough to the students, then a more obvious word could be used, such as *Coca-Cola*.

2. Pour aller des Etats-Unis en France on s'embarque
         A. à New York.
         B. à Southampton.
         C. au Havre.

Correct response: A

This item is intended to check the students' familiarity with the word *s'embarquer*. If the teacher feels that geography might prove a problem, a small map might be included.

**7.3.4** *Logical Inference*

After reading the key sentence, select which of the subsequent sentences
—A, B, or C—offers a logical explanation of or conclusion for the first
sentence.

Here is a sample item in English:

He goes to sleep.    A. He likes candy.
                     B. It's his favorite store.
                     C. He is tired.

Correct response: C—He goes to sleep *because* he is tired.

In order to select the correct response, the student must be familiar with
various structures and items of vocabulary.

Here are two sample items in German:

1. Die Berge sind weiß.    A. Sie sind mit Schnee bedeckt.
                           B. Das weiß ich nicht.
                           C. Sie sind weit von hier.

Correct response: A

Here the student must know the meaning of *weiß* as used in the first sentence and know the meanings of *Schnee* and *bedeckt*.

2. Man kann sich auf diese Uhr nicht verlassen.

       A. Wir finden diese Uhr sehr schön.
       B. Es ist vier Uhr.
       C. Die Uhr geht nicht richtig.

Correct reponse: C

In addition to understanding the use of the word *Uhr* in the first sentence,
the student must know the meaning of *sich verlassen* in order to select the
correct response.

**7.3.5** *Continuation of Thought*

This type of item is similar to item type 7.3.4, but the connection between the
two statements is logically less rigorous. The student is asked to select the
statement that best continues the thought of the first statement. Comprehension of such items generally depends on the recognition of familiar vocabulary
in a new context.

Here are two sample items in French:

1. Quel temps affreux!    A. Regardez comme il pleut.
                                      B. J'y vais de temps à autre.
                                      C. Il est déjà trois heures.

2. L'ascenseur est occupé.    A. Mais voici un fauteuil occupé.
                                         B. Il faut monter par l'escalier.
                                         C. L'armoire est très commode.

Correct responses: A, B

### 7.3.6   *Question and Answer*

For a class with experience in dialogues and directed conversations, question-answer items appear natural.

Here is a sample item in French:

Avez-vous fait une bonne pêche aujourd'hui?

     A. Non merci. Je préfère les poires.
     B. Mais oui. J'ai bien fait de prendre ce papier.
     C. C'était mieux que la semaine dernière.

Correct response: C

This reading item is based primarily on vocabulary: the meaning of the phrase *faire une bonne pêche*.

### 7.3.7   *Statement and Rejoinder*

In statement-rejoinder conversations, the rejoinders range in length from one word to several sentences. If the terms "statement" and "rejoinder" are not within the grasp of younger students, the teacher may word the directions as follows: select the statement another person would most likely make in continuing the conversation without changing the topic.

Here are two sample items in German:

1. Es zieht.    A. Ja, dieser Platz ist belegt.
                     B. Gestern ist sie abgefahren.
                     C. Ich werde das Fenster zumachen.

Correct response: C

To answer this item correctly, the student must know the expression *es zieht*.

2. Er bekommt immer schlechte Noten.

    A. Ich habe auch eine reiche Tante.
    B. Ja, aber er studiert wenig.
    C. Ich habe immer schrecklich viel zu tun.

Correct response: B

Notice that the only difference between the items of this section and the discrete listening-comprehension items lies in the presentation: listening skill vs. reading skill. If the teacher wants to evaluate student proficiency relative to these two skills, he might carry out the following experiment.

> Administer a test of twenty-five listening-comprehension items. Scramble the order of the items and administer the same test a week or so later in written form. Then correlate the overall student results and the item-by-item performances to determine whether the students are more proficient in reading or in listening.

## 7.4  TESTING OUTSIDE READING

The teacher will wish to determine how carefully the students have completed an outside reading assignment and whether they have understood what they read. Particularly with older students, a short quiz, announced or unannounced, at the beginning of the class hour will encourage conscientious preparation of homework.

### 7.4.1  *Multiple-Choice Items*

The multiple-choice reading quiz with corresponding answer sheet makes possible a quick check of student preparation. Question-answer items and true-false statements may be adapted. Students read the questions and options in the foreign language; this encourages them to increase their familiarity with the new words and expressions that appear in the text. Moreover, in a few minutes the teacher can cover the plot of a story or the factual information in a reading text, and the rest of the class period may be profitably spent in discussing the author's style or the general problems raised by the passage. The quiz itself can be graded very rapidly; if desired, students may exchange answer sheets and score themselves before the class discussion begins.

While such a quiz offers a good prelude to classwork and encourages better preparation, it has its limitations as a final examination. Challenging multiple-choice reading items with good distractors and four or five choices are difficult and time-consuming to prepare, and simple questions usually do not do justice to the readings.

### 7.4.2  *Written Questions*

According to the level of the class, very brief direct questions may be employed to verify whether all students have read and understood the assignment. Some precise questions of detail may be included to encourage closer reading of the text. The students write their answers either in English or in the target language.

### 7.4.3  *Written Summaries*

Students write a brief summary of the material they have read. If summaries are to be in the target language, this quiz technique should only be used with advanced students who possess a good command of the language.

## 7.5   DISCRETE GRAMMAR ITEMS

Multiple-choice items that evaluate passive knowledge of grammar are considered here as reading items. This type of discrete item is not recommended as a daily teaching device; for audio-lingual classes, pattern-type exercises are more effective in bringing the student to think in the foreign language. In a test the multiple-choice items allow the teacher to sample a large number of aspects in a relatively short time. Moreover, the scoring is rapid and objective.

Thus, it would appear that once the student has acquired the linguistic habit of saying "Ich gebe dem Mann das Buch," he should experience no difficulty with a test item such as:

Ich gebe _____ das Buch.     A. der  Mann
                                       B. des Mannes
                                       C. dem Mann
                                       D. den Mann

The item could also be worded:

Ich gebe _____ Mann das Buch.     A. der
                                     B. des
                                     C. dem
                                     D. den
                                     E. die

As the student reads the sentence, he mentally furnishes the correct form of the definite article. In a sense, such an item parallels the student's thought process in the foreign language: he first considers who is to receive the book—that is, the man—and then employs the proper form as a matter of of habit.

While it is true that the multiple-choice item may suggest a response that the student would not otherwise have thought of, this happens only rarely. Generally, even the slow students are aware of the forms of articles and pronouns and the existence of systems of inflection. Hesitation occurs when they realize that an article is required but the linguistic habit is not strong enough to enable them to make the correct choice.

Discrete reading items of the types suggested in this section have generally produced very reliable results. The teacher, however, must look at the objectives of his particular course to see which of the following types of questions would be valid for his class.

### 7.5.1   *Articles*

Since English has only one definite article orthographically, American students experience difficulty in learning the variety of definite articles in langauges such as French, German, Spanish, and Italian.

#### 7.5.1a   CHOICE OF DEFINITE ARTICLE

On your answer sheet indicate the proper articles to be used in each sentence. Use the following key: (A) le, (B) la, (C) l', (D) les.

1. Paul achète _____ livre.
2. Marie lit _____ histoire.
3. J'aime _____ pain.

Correct responses: A, C, A

A more informal item would have the student cross out the incorrect form:

Paul achète $\begin{array}{c} \text{le} \\ \text{la} \end{array}$ livre et Marie lit $\begin{array}{c} \text{l'} \\ \text{la} \end{array}$ histoire.

Such items are primarily vocabulary rather than usage items.

#### 7.5.1b   USE OF THE PARTITIVE

Complete the following sentences, using this key to indicate your answers: (A) le, (B) du, (C) de, (D) no word necessary.

1. Voulez-vous _____ pain?
2. Je n'aime pas manger trop _____ pain.
3. _____ pain (Pain) fait grossir.

Correct responses: B, C, A

Since all choices are of the same gender, the vocabulary element is minimized.

### 7.5.1c   FORM OF ARTICLE (SYNTAX)

Complete the following sentences, using this key to indicate your answers: (A) ein, (B) eines, (C) einem, (D) einen.

1. Da steht _____ Stuhl.
2. Ich kaufe meiner Mutter _____ Stuhl.
3. Legen Sie Ihren Hut auf _____ Stuhl!

Correct responses: A, D, D


### 7.5.1d   FORM OF ARTICLE: INDIVIDUAL ITEMS

Complete the following German sentence:

Der Wagen _____ fährt gut.    A. der Vater
                                               B. des Vaters
                                               C. dem Vater
                                               D. den Vater

Correct response: B


### 7.5.2   *Adjectives*

In an inflected language, items similar to those above may be used to test the use of adjectives. Here are some sample items in German.

### 7.5.2a   SERIES ITEMS

Complete the following sentences, using this key to indicate your responses: (A) sein, (B) seine, (C) seines, (D) seiner.

1. Herr Müller ist _____ Lehrer.
2. Er kennt _____ Studenten.
3. Das war _____ Frage.

Correct responses: A, B, B

### 7.5.2b   DISCRETE ITEMS

Complete the following sentence:

Wie _____ Samstag füttert Frau Lehmann die Enten.    A. jeder
                                                                        B. jeden
                                                                         C. jedem
                                                                          D. jedes

Correct response: B

### 7.5.3 *Pronouns*

#### 7.5.3a PERSONAL PRONOUNS

Complete the following sentence:

Geben Sie _____ zwei Paar Strümpfe!

- A. ich
- B. mir
- C. mich
- D. zu mir

Correct response: B

#### 7.5.3b DOUBLE-CHOICE ITEMS

In the use of pronouns, a foreign language often makes distinctions that do not exist in English; students consequently tend to confuse the pronouns used in such expressions. The teacher may test the student's knowledge of pronoun usage with an item like the one below, using four options to make the item more reliable. (Note: The student must have both pronouns correct in order to receive credit for the item.)

Complete the following sentences:

Connaissez-vous Marcel Dupont? _____ professeur maintenant. _____ un très bon professeur, dit-on.

- A. C'est, C'est
- B. C'est, Il est
- C. Il est, C'est
- D. Il est, Il est

Correct response: C

#### 7.5.3c RELATIVE PRONOUNS

Complete the following sentences, using this key to indicate your responses: (A) que, (B) quien, (C) quienes, (D) no word necessary.

1. Es el libro de _____ hablamos ayer.
2. Ese es el amo del perro _____ llamó.
3. Son los amigos con _____ hablaba.

Correct responses: A, B, C

Here is a sentence-completion item in French:

Voilà une femme que
- A. je me souviens.
- B. nous connaît.
- C. je connais.
- D. se souvient de moi.

Correct response: C

The preceding item evaluates student familiarity with relative pronouns and with the constructions using *se souvenir de* and *connaître*.

### 7.5.4 *Prepositions*

If the target language uses prepositions in constructions where English does not, or if the choice of prepositions is not the same in both languages, conflict develops. Familiarity with prepositions and their use may be easily tested with multiple-choice items.

Here are some sample items in French:

Complete the following sentences, using this key to indicate your responses: (A) à, (B) de (d'), (C) pour, (D) no word necessary.

1. Il nous remercie _____ avoir téléphoné.
2. J'apprends à mon frère _____ nager.
3. Je n'ose pas _____ l'inviter.

Correct responses: B, A, D

### 7.5.5 *Conjunctions*

#### 7.5.5a CHOICE AMONG SUPPLIED CONJUNCTIONS

Complete the following sentences, using this key to indicate your responses: (A) als, (B) wenn, (C) wann.

1. _____ bist du hier angekommen?
2. _____ ich ankam, war mein Bruder schon da.
3. Gehen wir, _____ es morgen regnet?

Correct responses: C, A, B

#### 7.5.5b DISCRIMINATION AMONG CONJUNCTIONS

Indicate which of the following conjunctions may *not* be substituted for the underlined conjunction unless other changes in the sentence are made.

Il me donne un cadeau <u>quand</u> je suis sage.
    A. puisque
    B. parce que
    C. pour que
    D. lorsque

Correct response: C

### 7.5.6  *Word Order*

The word at the left belongs somewhere in the sentence that follows it. Indicate which letter in parentheses corresponds to the place where the word should be inserted and blacken the corresponding space on your answer sheet.

Here are two sample items in German:

1. nicht     Ich (A) werde (B) das Buch (C) lesen (D).
2. mir       Er (A) wollte (B) ihn (C) geben (D).

Correct responses: C, C

### 7.5.7  *Verbs*

#### 7.5.7a  MODE

When certain indicative and subjunctive forms are identical, as is the case in French, items can be constructed to check the student's active knowledge of grammatical usage.

Determine whether the underlined verb is in the subjunctive or in the indicative. Indicate your answer as follows:  A = | subjunctive |, B = | indicative |.

1. Il faut qu'ils <u>viennent</u> demain.
2. Je ne veux pas qu'elle <u>donne</u> le livre à sa mère.
3. Nous pensons qu'elle <u>étudie</u> trop.

Correct responses: A, A, B

#### 7.5.7b  SEQUENCE OF TENSES

Complete the following sentence:

Quand vous _____ fini, passez chez moi.     A. êtes
                                                            B. serez
                                                            C. avez
                                                            D. aurez

Correct response: D

Here is another format in French:

J'achèterai un manteau quand     A. je vais en ville.
                                                                      B. j'allais en ville.
                                                                      C. je suis allé en ville.
                                                                      D. j'irai en ville.

Correct response: D

**7.5.8**   *Question and Answer*

A variety of grammatical material may be tested through discrete question-and-answer items. The French sample item below evaluates knowledge of verb forms and reflexive pronouns and general comprehension.

Est-ce que je vous dérange?      A.  Oui, je me dérange.

                                 B.  Oui, je vous dérange.

                                 C.  Oui, vous me dérangez.

                                 D.  Oui, vous vous dérangez.

Correct response: C

## 7.6   DISCRETE VOCABULARY ITEMS

Most reading tests directly or indirectly measure the student's familiarity with the words and the idioms of the foreign language. Short vocabulary items request the student to choose a synonym or an antonym from the three or four words given. Some ask for a definition in the target language. Often, longer reading items hinge not so much on general reading skill but on knowledge of a particular word. Except in tests for advanced students, teachers of audio-lingual classes should not encourage excessive translation from the target language into English by using English in the vocabulary items. It is particularly inadvisable to reinforce the dangerous tendency to establish word-for-word equivalents between English and the target language.

In preparing discrete tests based on vocabulary, the teacher should take care to see that the comprehension problem lies in one place, either in the stem or in the options. If the difficult vocabulary item is in the stem, all students should understand the meaning of the options. It is generally better to present the key word in a sentence with just enough context to limit the meaning of the word, but not too much to give away the right answer. If the problem lies in the choice of options, the meaning of the stem should be evident to all.

**7.6.1**   *Synonyms*

Indicate which of the following words is closest in meaning to the underlined word (or words) in the sentence.

Here is a sample item in French:

Monique assiste au cours d'anglais.      A.  est présente

                                         B.  aide le professeur

                                         C.  est professeur

                                         D.  regarde le professeur

Correct response: A

In this item, A is the correct choice. Option B is a form distractor: the French word *assiste* looks like the English *assist*, meaning to help or aid (hence *aide*). Option C is a content distractor: since the sentence mentions an English class, perhaps the student would think that *assiste* means *teaches*. Option D is a meaning distractor, similar in function to the correct response.[1]

### 7.6.2 *Antonyms*

Indicate which of the following words is closest to meaning the *opposite* of the underlined word(s) in the sentence.

Here is a sample item in French:

Jean se met à son travail.    A. n'organise pas
                                       B. veut quitter
                                       C. termine
                                       D. a faim pendant

Correct response: C

### 7.6.3 *Definition*

The stem of this Spanish item best defines which of the following words:

el habitante de una colonia    A. Colón
                                       B. el colono
                                       C. el colon
                                       D. el coloniaje

Correct response: B

In a variation of this item type, the student must choose the appropriate definition of the underlined word.

Here is a sample item in German:

Er will seinen Vater umbringen.    A. zum Flughafen fahren
                                       B. holen
                                       C. töten
                                       D. besuchen

Correct response: C

### 7.6.4 *Completion*

The student is asked to complete a sentence by selecting the omitted word. Such items are effective in measuring his familiarity with certain idiomatic

---

[1] For more details on the selection of distractors in vocabulary items, see Robert Lado, *Language Testing* (New York: McGraw-Hill, 1964), pp. 191–97.

phrases. Occasionally it is possible to construct a series of items based on the same options.

Here are some sample items in French:

> Complete the following sentences, using this key to indicate your choice:
> (A) a, (B) est, (C) fait, (D) va.

> 1. Comment _____ ta mère; est-elle encore malade?
> 2. Elle supporte mal la chaleur et il _____ très chaud.
> 3. Bien sûr, Paul _____ toujours raison.

Correct responses: D, C, A

More often, separate choices may be prepared for each item.

Here are two sample items in German:

> 1. Wir _____ ihm für seinen Brief.    A. denken
>                                                B. danken
>                                                C. glauben

> 2. Am Sonntag ist das Klassenzimmer _____.    A. leer
>                                                          B. heiß
>                                                         C. spät

Correct responses: B, A

## 7.7  PASSAGE ITEMS

Passage items are among the best-known reading tests. However, the teacher must take care to make sure that the questions accompanying the passage are genuine reading-comprehension items, for there is the possibility that students could answer some poorly constructed items without having read the text. Reading-comprehension items are best pretested on individuals who have not read the accompanying passage.

### 7.7.1  *Printed Options*

In the pure reading test, the student reads both questions and answers and selects the correct responses from the options given. Such reading-comprehension passages were for many years the mainstay of the College Boards and the New York State Regents examinations.

#### 7.7.1a  TRUE-FALSE

For elementary—and often intermediate—students, short passages with true-false sentences may be used as informal classroom tests. Care must be taken that the statements do not turn into exercises in logical thinking and problem solving.

Here is a sample passage in French:

> Les enfants ne sont pas encore levés parce qu'ils se sont couchés tard hier soir. Mais nous sommes au mois de juillet et il n'y a pas d'école. Alors les enfants n'ont pas besoin de se lever de très bonne heure.

After you have read the above passage, decide whether the following statements are true or false. Indicate your answer as follows: A = | true |, B = | false |.

1. Les enfants sont encore couchés.
2. Ils ont classe demain.
3. L'école commence en juillet.

Correct responses: A, B, B

### 7.7.1b VARIED QUESTIONS

The following passage in French could be administered as a reading test to more advanced students:

> Je suis venue à Livry achever (1) les beaux jours, et dire adieu aux feuilles; elles sont encore toutes aux arbres; elles (2) n'ont fait que changer (3) de couleur: au lieu d'être vertes, elles sont aurores (4)...

After you have read the above passage, answer the following questions:

1. Qui est l'auteur?    A. une femme
                        B. un homme
                        C. ou un homme ou une femme

Correct response: A

To answer this item correctly, the students must understand the importance of the final *e* of *venue*.

2. (1) veut dire    A. admirer.
                    B. réussir.
                    C. finir.

Correct response: C

This is a vocabulary item; B is a form distractor because *achever* looks like the English *achieve*, i.e., *réussir*.

3. (2) se rapporte aux    A. jours.
                          B. feuilles.
                          C. arbres.

Correct response: B

Item 7.7.1b.3 tests whether the student has correctly identified the antecedent of the pronoun *elles*.

4. (3) est l'équivalent de     A. ont seulement changé.
                                     B. doivent changer.
                                     C. n'ont pas encore changé.

Correct response: A

To select the proper response for this comprehension item, the student must be familiar with *ne . . . que* and this particular use of *faire*.

5. Dans le texte, (4) représente     A. un phénomène lumineux.
                                        B. le lever du soleil.
                                        C. une couleur.

Correct response: C

In this item the student demonstrates his ability to select the proper definition of a word according to the context in which it is used. The item could be made a little more difficult if Option C were to read *un teint*.

### 7.7.1c USE OF AVAILABLE TESTS

It is rather time-consuming to prepare passages followed by a variety of multiple-choice items. Often, however, it is possible to procure old copies or samples of New York Regents or College Board examinations. The items could be modified to meet the needs of the students. However, copyrights and permissions must first be checked.

### 7.7.2 *Written Answers*

For classroom use, reading tests with questions to be answered in writing are often more efficient than multiple-choice tests because they can be prepared in less time. However, the teacher must realize that two skills, reading and writing, are involved in such a test. Two grades could be assigned: one for comprehension (correct content) and one for written expression (correct form).

An unfamiliar passage, depending on its content, lends itself to a variety of item types:

Definition of underlined words or expressions

Evaluation of aptness of certain words or expressions: Why did the author use this word in the text rather than . . . ?

Brief résumé of the passage

What is the attitude of the author toward his subject? How is that attitude expressed?

Does the passage reflect the point of view of one of the characters? Which one? How is the reader made aware of this? (for fiction passages)

The range of questions will be limited by the teacher's objectives and by the level of the class. Elementary students will write only short summaries or answer questions that require more or less a restatement of the passage. The types of questions asked of more advanced students will be determined by their vocabulary and their background. If the writing sample contains too many mistakes (other than spelling), the teacher should review the difficult structures and vocabulary in class. On the next test the questions should be modified so that the students are encouraged to use expressions they know and can handle accurately.

### 7.7.3 *Oral Answers*

For informal classroom use, it is possible to combine comprehension passages with oral responses. The passage may be given to the students for a stated length of time; they are asked to prepare an oral résumé or to prepare oral answers for specific questions.

If such a passage is used as a laboratory test, all students will record their responses simultaneously on their tapes. If the teacher must see students individually, they should be allowed equal preparation time. Thus, while Student A answers the questions, Student B may read the text; as Student B recites, Student C is given the text, and so on. Those not being tested could be given a written assignment. In scoring such a test, the teacher must determine from his course objective what percentage of the grade is allotted to reading comprehension and what percentage to speaking ability (fluency, pronunciation, correctness, etc.).

## 7.8. READING SPEED

Speed is one of the features that clearly distinguish the reading skill from the other three skills. Rapidity of writing or speaking is limited by the muscular functioning of the hand or the speech organs; rapidity of listening comprehension is determined by the speed at which others speak. Only in reading can the mind assimilate information in much less time than that required for writing it down.

As the student learns to read the target language, he gradually develops speed in reading; the advanced student should be able to read the target language as quickly as his native English. Even the intermediate student should be able to read appropriate texts with maximum direct association. Fluency in reading is a sign that the student is not mentally transposing the text partially or entirely into English.[1]

---

[1] Consult George A. C. Scherer *et al.*, "Reading for Meaning," in *Northeast Conference Reports of the Working Committees*, William Bottiglia, ed., 1963, pp. 23–60.

**7.8.1**  *Speed and Comprehension Tests*

The standardized commercial tests are timed. The student receives a score that indicates the number of comprehension questions he has answered correctly in the allotted time; in order to discourage indiscriminate guessing, some tests employ a modified scoring system (see Section 4.5). The teacher can determine a time limit for his own reading-comprehension tests if he so desires. Another possibility is to note the time at which each student finishes the test; with older students, each one may record his finishing time on the back of his paper.

**7.8.2**  *Pure Speed Tests*

A pure speed test may be constructed as follows: select a long passage appropriate to the reading level of the majority of the class. At uneven intervals insert nonsense words—words that are very obviously out of context. As the student reads the passage he crosses out the nonsense words.

A mimeographed copy of the text is placed face-down on each desk. At the signal, the students turn over the papers and start reading, pencil in hand. When time is called, the teacher can quickly assess each student's reading speed by scanning the paper to see how many words have been crossed out.

Here is a sample passage in Spanish, showing how far a student had read before being told to stop:

Fig. 19

```
Había una vieja que tenía dos perros:  el uno se llamaba
Hueso y el otro, Pellejo.  En su dormitorio la vieja voy
tenía una gran caja llena de dinero que estaba siempre
cerrada con llave.  Un día la viejita las salió de su casa
con los perros y como siempre  no dejó la llave en casa.
Mientras estaban fuera, llegó un cuántos ladrón y se metió
debajo de la cama.  La buena señora volvió por la noche y
se preparó para acostarse qué.  El ladrón, que estaba espe-
rando debajo de la cama, no hacía ningún ruido.  Pensaba
que una vez que se durmiera, él podría robarle la llave y
escaparse con el dinero.  Pero al meter los zapatos debajo
de la cama, la viejita vio los pies andar del ladrón.  Y
como todas las viejas son muy listas, ésta también lo era.
Y entonces empezó a lamentarse en voz puerta baja diciendo:
--Ya estoy muy vieja; ay, ya estoy muy vieja y muy flaca;
estoy sólo hueso y pellojo--.  Y repetía cada vez más
enérgica y firme --¡hueso y pellejo!, ¡hueso cama y pelle-
jo!--  Y en ese momento, los perros la oyeron y vinieron
corriendo porque creían que los llamaba.  Ella les hizo una
seña y los perros se echaron sobre el otros ladrón ha-
ciéndole pedazos.[1]
```

[1] Text from *A-LM Spanish: Level Two* (New York: Harcourt, Brace & World, 1961), p. 179.

# CHAPTER EIGHT
# THE WRITING TEST

Of the four language skills, writing may truly be considered the most sophisticated. In listening and in reading, the student receives a message formulated by another; his role is passive even though he may be mentally interpreting and analyzing what he is hearing or reading. In speaking, the student is engaged in communicating his own ideas and feelings, but with approximations and explanations; conversation involves give-and-take with an interlocutor. Communication through the written word, on the other hand, possesses a certain degree of finality and demands real proficiency from the writer if it is to be effective. Many American college students have not even mastered the art of writing English, their native language.

The student learning a foreign language follows a series of steps in developing the writing skill. The mechanics—vocabulary, spelling, grammar—must be mastered before the student can aspire to precision of expression, fluency, and style. Tests must consequently be so structured that they measure the various aspects of student progress toward the acquisition of this fourth skill.

## 8.1 GENERAL CONSIDERATIONS

Historically, writing was not a transcription of the spoken language but an independent system of visual communication. Pictorial symbols or hieroglyphs, such as those used by the ancient Egyptians and the American Indians, were gradually replaced by more abstract forms of writing that eventually attempted to represent the spoken language. This transition, though still incomplete, has passed through three major stages: [1]

*Characters* are formal items, such as those used in classical Chinese (which possesses from five to six thousand commonly used characters); even English uses certain characters such as % and &.

*Syllabaries,* containing from fifty to five thousand symbols, note consonant articulations and indicate vowels, when necessary, by a system of dots or other marks. This partly phonological type of writing is characteristic of the ancient Semitic languages, such as Hebrew and Arabic, several languages of India, and Javanese. Japanese combines characters (borrowed from the Chinese) with a syllabic script.

*Alphabets,* invented in ancient Greece, use well under fifty single symbols to represent all consonant and vowel sounds. They are the easiest script to learn and to use; even Chinese is changing very slowly to a phonological system based on the Roman alphabet.

The phonological scripts—syllabaries and, particularly, alphabets—are imperfect transcriptions of the spoken language; stress and intonation are shown in a sketchy manner if at all. While spelling and pronunciation are quite close in Italian, English has an extremely ambiguous spelling system, and French writing reveals many vestigial sounds that are no longer pronounced. Since the invention of printing, the written language has exercised a conservative influence over the speech community. The continual evolution of the spoken language is counteracted by the presence of the "correct" forms in newspapers, magazines, and books.

Written language possesses its own conventions, which in certain cases do not parallel the spoken language. Sometimes the written language is entirely different from the spoken language; note the use of Latin in the Middle Ages or the use of English, French, or Swahili by many African tribesmen who speak other dialects. In French, the *passé simple* may be considered uniquely a written form.

What are the problems encountered by the American student learning to to write the target language? What particular aspects of the writing skill should the teacher test and evaluate?

Almost all American students learning to write a foreign language are literate in English. They know the Roman alphabet, even though they have

[1] See R. H. Robbins, *General Linguistics* (Bloomington: Indiana University Press, 1965), pp. 121–25.

learned to equate letters and letter combinations with English sounds. They realize, from their experience in spelling, that a written language can be a very imperfect transcription of the spoken language. One letter or cluster of letters can represent a variety of sounds (for example, *tough, bough, though, thought*); consequently, Americans do not think it strange when they find a similar phenomenon in French (bi*en*, r*enne, en,* parl*ent*). Moreover, they realize that one sound may be transcribed in a number of ways (English: *soul, sole;* French: *fin, faim*). They adapt even more happily to a language with a more phonological writing system, such as Spanish or Russian (in spite of the new accent marks of the former and the modified alphabet of the latter).

Furthermore, American students are familiar with certain morphemes in both their oral and written forms. On the printed page they recognize *'s* as a sign of possession, even though in spoken English they listen for /s/ (as in *Pat's*), /z/ (as in *Sal's*), and /ɪz/ (as in *Gus's*). A morphological consistency in spelling coupled with an inconsistency in the spoken language is nothing new; they are not surprised to encounter such features in other languages. Students recognize the importance of the morphological features of the printed language and should be tested in their mastery of them.

The commonly taught foreign languages possess, as does English, a rapid spoken form that is not transcribed phonetically in writing. Many Americans say "Ya gonna come?" but write "Are you going to come?" Similarly, whereas many Germans say something that sounds like "Chaps nicht," they write "Ich habe es nicht."

English uses punctuation marks to separate elements of the sentence. Other languages have slightly different systems of punctuation that must be learned. The rules of punctuation in German are strict but the marks are fairly similar to English marks; punctuation rules in Spanish are freer but there are new symbols to be learned. In all writing exercises, the proper use of punctuation should be stressed.

Each language possesses certain typographical conventions that are quite evident—in business letters, for example; certain types of spacing, punctuation, and margins are used in each country. Written conventions also exist: salutations and closings. These elements, totally independent of the spoken language, must be learned. Written conventions exist in other specialized areas, too—in law, medicine, science, and so on.

The conservative nature of the written language explains the stricter conventions and the narrow margin of tolerance that educated natives have in regard to inaccuracies in writing. A heavy "foreign" accent, if it does not greatly interfere with comprehension, is permitted and is sometimes appreciated (note the success of Maurice Chevalier), but a letter poorly worded or containing misspellings elicits a negative reaction. The student and the teacher must strive for perfection in the writing skill. In audio-lingual classes, the students are encouraged to write only words and phrases they can handle accurately and easily. Written tests should enable the student to demonstrate his proficiency. In a well-prepared test, the mistakes should be few.

## 8.2  PREPARATION AND SCORING

From the outset, writing quizzes, even simple copying tests, should be strictly graded. Since in audio-lingual classes vocabulary and structure are first presented and mastered orally, the later emphasis in writing should be on perfection.

In preparing the writing test, the teacher must determine what elements are to be evaluated and the relative importance of various sections of the test. A carefully planned test can be graded rapidly.

**8.2.1**  *Sample Writing Test: Levels One and Two*

Let us look at a brief writing test in French and analyze the scoring system. The items used are directed sentences (see Section 8.6).

Fig. 20

Writing Test

A. Replace the underlined word with the new pronoun and make all other related changes.

    1. Jean se lève tôt.  Nous _____.

    2. Marie étudie ses leçons.  Vous _____.

    3. Je travaille chez mon frère.  Il _____.

    4. Tu vas te faire mal.  Je _____.

    5. Vous vous appelez Pierre.  Tu _____.

B. Rewrite each of the following sentences using the future tense.

    6. Je viens à deux heures.  Demain _____.

    7. Il fait les courses.  Demain _____.

    8. Nous vendons nos livres.  Demain _____.

    9. Vous finissez cette lecture.  Demain _____.

    10. Tu donnes le billet.  Demain _____.

Correct responses: 1. Nous nous levons tôt. 2. Vous étudiez vos leçons. 3. Il travaille chez son frère. 4. Je vais me faire mal. 5. Tu t'appelles Pierre. 6. Demain je viendra . . . 7. Demain il fera . . . 8. Demain nous viendrons . . . 9. Demain vous finirez . . . 10. Demain tu donneras . . .

Note that this sample test differs from a pattern drill in that no models, only the directions, are given. The first part of the quiz constitutes a quick review of verbs with an irregular present tense, of reflexives, and of possessive pronouns. If classroom drill on each type of problem has been sufficient, the students should perform well on the mixed questions. The second part tests the structures currently being studied in the class: the forms of the future tense.

The scoring may be outlined as follows.

Section A   Each sentence is valued at 3 points:
1 point for the stem of the verb
1 point for the verb ending
1 point for the additional change to be made

The highest possible score for this section would be 15 points. (In another scoring system, both verb stem and verb ending could be valued at ½ point, particularly if this part of the test constitutes a review of known material; in this case the highest possible score would be 10 points.)

Section B   Each sentence is valued at 2 points:
1 point for the stem of the verb
1 point for the verb ending

The highest possible score for this section would be 10 points. Consequently, the maximum score for the whole quiz would be 25 (or 20) points; letter grades could be assigned at the discretion of the teacher.

This system of divided scoring, which assigns 2 points to one word—the verb in the above case—enables the teacher to assess student progress more effectively. If all the errors are recorded in two (or three) columns, the teacher can see at a glance if the class as a whole needs additional drill on a specific aspect of the material being tested.

From the table the teacher can see that his students need additional work on the reflexive pronouns and on the singular verb endings for the future tense. Such a table is even more useful in analyzing results of a longer test or of large numbers of students; in most cases the teacher can, with practice, mentally appraise the results of a short test given to a small class.

| Table of errors | | | |
|---|---|---|---|
| Sentence | Verb | | Other |
| | stem | ending | |
| 1 | // | | 卌 / |
| 2 | / | | // |
| 3 | | | /// |
| 4 | / | / | 卌 /// |
| 5 | /// | // | 卌 |
| 6 | /// | 卌 | |
| 7 | //// | 卌 // | |
| 8 | | / | |
| 9 | // | | |
| 10 | | 卌 / | |

FIG. 21

### 8.2.2  *The Writing Test with Spoken Cues*

Giving a written test with oral cues permits a high degree of class efficiency. The rate at which the items are read determines the speed at which the students must work; consequently, the whole class finishes at the same time. If the test is to be administered to several sections, the spoken cues may be taped in advance; the teacher is then free to proctor while students are taking the quiz.

In preparing the written test with oral cues, the teacher must not only select the appropriate items but also consider how he will score the following:

Comprehension. Does the student's answer show he has understood the meaning of the sentence?

Spelling. Has the student understood the sentence, but simply misspelled certain words? Do the misspellings alter the meaning of the sentence?

Morphology. Has the student mastered the structures being tested? Has he mastered all the aspects of each structure?

If this test with oral cues is to be considered a *written* test, then the content must be familiar to all the students. A student with low proficiency in listening comprehension may fail to understand a sentence; his subsequent errors in spelling and morphology would not provide a reliable indication of his mastery of the skill of writing.

**8.2.3**  *Scoring Dictation*

In scoring dictations the teacher should realize that the major consideration is not so much the manner in which points are assigned, but rather the consistent use of a given scoring system.

**8.2.3a**  SCORING BY WORDS

The basic unit of scoring can be the individual printed word. Only one error per word should be counted, for the student who omits a word should not be penalized less than the one who tries to write the word and makes several mistakes. Various word-unit scoring systems exist. The most common include:

1. 1 point off for each incorrect or omitted word;
2. ½ point off for each recognizable word with a spelling error, 1 point off for each omitted or unrecognizable word;
3. ¼ point off for a wrong or omitted accent, ½ point off for a misspelled but recognizable word, 1 point off for each omitted or unrecognizable word;
4. like 3, but with 1 point off for a word containing a morphological error, such as an incorrect verb or adjective ending.

Generally a recurring word consistently misspelled counts as only one error.

System 1 places the emphasis on perfection: the student who has a word *almost* right receives no more credit than the student who omitted the word. Systems 3 and 4 are more detailed, and scoring according to these systems takes more time. It is recommended that the teacher select one system and employ it for all dictations so that by comparing performances he may reliably assess the progress of the class and the improvement of the individual student during the semester or year.

**8.2.3b**  SCORING BY PHRASES

On the scorer's copy, the dictation may be divided into words or phrases. Within this framework, scoring variations may be devised similar to systems 1 through 4 above.

Here is a sample in French:

Hier * / nous avons vu / nos grands-parents / qui demeurent / à la campagne. / J'ai joué / avec mon cousin, / Henri,* / qui aime jouer / au football.

* Score ½ point for this word and other similarly marked words or groups. Score 1 point for each of the other groups.[1]

[1] Taken from Harry L. Bratnober, *Teachers' Guide, Recorded Text and Key for Test Tapes to Accompany New First-Year French, New Junior French by O'Brien and Lafrance* (Boston: Ginn, 1964), p. 28.

## 8.3   PRE-WRITING TESTS

In order to write a foreign language, the student must first be familiar with the graphemes (the alphabet or characters) in which that language is transcribed. Since the most commonly taught languages, such as Spanish, French, and German, employ the Roman alphabet, the student must learn only certain accent marks or an occasional new letter or digraph. If the target language is Russian, a greatly modified alphabet must be learned; in the case of Chinese, a new and voluminous set of characters is to be mastered.

The assimilation of these mechanical aspects of writing entails practice and drill. The potential monotony of this type of learning may be avoided by the introduction of frequent brief tests.

### 8.3.1   *Copying*

The student is graded on his accuracy in copying characters or sentences. The teacher must be extremely strict in demanding a perfect copy. Both spelling and punctuation should be checked.

#### 8.3.1a   SCRIPT WRITING: ACCURACY

The student is given a printed sentence which he is to write in script.

#### 8.3.1b   SCRIPT WRITING: SPEED

The student is given a limited period (perhaps three minutes) in which to copy a printed paragraph or paragraphs in script. If the student finishes before time is called he should begin copying the paragraph again. The work is graded on the basis of the length of the material copied and accuracy.

### 8.3.2   *Dictation: Words and Phrases*

The teacher reads in the new language words or phrases that the student is to write. At this elementary level, it is essential that the student be familiar with the text so that no problem of comprehension exists.

To provide the desirable reinforcement, these dictation tests should be corrected immediately; good results are often obtained by having the students exchange papers with one another. To save class time, the teacher could distribute mimeographed copies of the dictation or raise a wall chart to uncover the correct words or phrases, written before class on the blackboard.

## 8.4 DICTATION

Dictation, in which the student transcribes a passage he hears read (live or on tape), is used to some extent by almost all language teachers. In audio-lingual classes, exercises in dictation give the student practice in associating the sounds of the new language with their written form; they are employed, as we have seen, in effecting the transition from the listening and speaking skills to the reading and writing skills.

Foreign-language specialists, however, are not in agreement about the ef-fectiveness of the dictation as an examination for more advanced students. It is evident that the art of taking dictation is a specialized skill. Sentences are read slowly and are clearly enunciated; consequently, emphasis, in most languages, falls on phonemic discrimination. In Spanish, Italian, and Russian the "fit" between sounds and letters is quite close. In a language such as French, however, the student must clearly comprehend the passage in order to make the required morphological distinctions. Therefore, in France the *dictée* is widely used in place of word-list spelling tests because in taking dictation the students must also exhibit their awareness of grammar. A dicta-tion also reveals the students' knowledge of punctuation.

In spite of its artificiality the dictation has retained a place of high favor in the opinion of many language teachers. Whatever the dictation lacks theoretically, dictation scores in practice correlate very well with overall language achievement. One recent study seems to indicate that unless students receive a great deal of dictation work in class, the score on a final dictation correlates highly with the score on a full-length examination testing the skills of listening, reading, and writing.[1] Although more research is needed to ar-rive at a precise definition of the merits and deficiencies of dictation tests, such tests continue to be widely used in the language classroom.

### 8.4.1 *Types of Dictations*

#### 8.4.1a PARTIAL OR SPOT DICTATION

In a partial dictation each student receives a copy of a passage in which function words, or often merely prefixes and endings, have been left out. As he listens to the passage being read, he fills in the blanks. Such dictations, while necessitating a certain amount of advance preparation, have two distinct advantages. First, they can be administered more rapidly and scored more objectively than conventional dictations. Second, they permit the teacher to test only the problem areas; students do not waste time writing words and phrases that they already handle relatively accurately.

[1] See R. Valette, "The Use of the *Dictée* in the French Language Classroom," *Modern Language Journal*, Vol. XLVIII (November 1964), pp. 431–34.

### 8.4.1b   PREPARED DICTATION

The dictation is taken directly from a dialogue or selection that the student has previously prepared. Such a dictation is generally employed when the writing skill is being introduced. If announced in advance, it may produce scores which fail to correlate with general language achievement: conscientious students with very poor oral discrimination may obtain a high score by memorizing the passage to be tested.

If the teacher wishes to measure retention and familiarity with patterns, each sentence may be read only once and at normal speed. This is particularly effective with older students.

### 8.4.1c   PARAPHRASED DICTATION

The dictation is a paraphrase of a dialogue or selection which the student has previously studied. Patterns and vocabulary remain the same, but the wording is modified in order not to favor the student who tends to memorize dictation material. The results on this type of dictation are of greater validity in demonstrating language achievement than those obtained from prepared dictation.

The sentences in this type of dictation may be read only once or twice at normal speed.

### 8.4.1d   DICTATION OF NEW MATERIAL

Such tests, which may be used for intermediate and advanced students, offer the most reliable and most valid measure of student skill in dictation.

### 8.4.2   *Giving the Dictation*

When a test dictation is given, certain precautions must be taken to make sure that the test is always administered in the same manner. Only in this way can the teacher make valid comparisons between the performances of different classes or of the same student on different occasions.

Here is one effective technique of administering a test dictation. First, the whole passage is read at normal speed. The students are told not to write, just to listen carefully. Then the passage is read a phrase at a time, with pauses during which the students write down what they have heard. At this time the teacher may read each phrase either once or twice, as long as he is consistent. (At the teacher's discretion, punctuation marks may be given in the target language.) Finally, the entire passage is read again at normal speed, and the students are given a few minutes for final revision. It is imperative that the teacher *never* repeat a particular phrase at a student's request.

The dictation may also be administered in the language laboratory. If the tape is to be played from a master console, the dictation script should be prerecorded in the manner described above. If each student is to play his own tape, the dictation passage could be recorded only once, at normal speed. In that case, the student may be allowed as much time as he needs to take down the passage; he may stop, rewind, and replay phrases as often as necessary. Scores from this latter type of test (power test) may be compared with each other, but not with scores from the former (partial speed test).

For suggestions on scoring dictations, see Section 8.2.3.

## 8.5  PARTIAL SENTENCES

Partial-sentence items require the student to complete the phrases given in the test booklet. Partial sentences differ, however, from certain "traditional" fill-in-the-blank items in the following two ways. First, partial sentences are *not* sentences written in a mixture of the two languages. Nothing more effectively defeats the goals of audio-lingual classes and the intentions of any language teacher eager to have the students develop fluency in the target language than hybrid sentences such as: Ich gehe _____ (home). Nous _____ (have just bought) une maison. Haga el favor de _____ (study) la lección.

Much later in the student's instruction, when translation becomes a legitimate goal, items such as those in Section 8.10 may be considered. But even at that time, test sentences should *never* be given in which two languages are mixed.

Second, at the elementary levels, it is better to avoid partial-sentence items in which the verb to be employed is presented in the infinitive, such as: Pierre _____ (venir) chez moi. Student dependence on the infinitive is unnatural and should not be encouraged. If verb forms are to be evaluated, directed sentences (8.6) may be used effectively.

With these considerations in mind, let us examine possible partial sentences.

### 8.5.1  *Prefixes and Endings*

This type of writing test tends to be artificial and should only be used, if at all, with advanced students.

Here are some sample items:

Fill in the blanks in the following sentences:

1. Nous sommes all____ en ville.
2. Die Kinder geh____ zur Schule.
3. Los automóviles blanc____ son de los Estados Unidos.

Correct responses: allé(e)s, gehen, blancos

### 8.5.2 *"Little" Words*

Entire words may be left out of sentences if the student can easily deduce which elements must be added. However, this type of item should not be reduced to a guessing game or an exercise in puzzle-solving. The sentences could be composed to form an entire paragraph.

Here are some isolated sample items:

1. Chantal veut aller _____ Etats-Unis.
2. Die Frau hat eine schlimme Wunde _____ Kopf.
3. Son _____ diez menos cuarto.
4. Sandro ha fatto _____ viaggio molto bello.

Correct responses: aux, am, las, uno

### 8.5.3 *Phrases or Clauses (Dehydrated Clauses)*

If a phrase or clause is omitted, the item contains words to be used in finishing the sentence. Such items are very effective for testing word order and sequence of tenses.

Here are some sample items:

1. J'ai peur que _____ (Marie / venir / maintenant)
2. Ich weiß, daß _____ (Vater / sein / krank)
3. En realidad José era un hombre _____ (preferir / hacer / nada)

Possible responses: Marie ne vienne maintenant; Vater krank ist; que prefirió no hacer nada

## 8.6   DIRECTED SENTENCES

An important step in the acquisition of the writing skill is learning to write sentences. At first this practice is carefully structured so that the students will produce accurate and natural sentences. Most audio-lingual pattern drills may be adapted to written testing. Since the purpose of pattern practice is to enable the student to handle certain forms automatically, this type of test should be employed after the patterns have been given considerable drill. It must be remembered that if a complicated cue is given orally, listening comprehension becomes an unwanted factor. If, on the other hand, the initial phrase is printed, very simple patterns may become mere copying exercises. Other more specialized items, appropriate only to the skill of writing, are also effective in testing the student's ability to construct directed sentences within predetermined limitations.

The following sample items show how structural patterns may be used in written classroom tests.

### 8.6.1 *Simple Substitution*

The student replaces one element in the sentence with another.

Here is a sample item in French:

Je vais en ville.   (à la campagne)
Je vais à la campagne.

This type of test may be considered a variation of the pre-writing dictation. Comprehension should pose no problem; the student is thus free to concentrate on spelling.

### 8.6.2 *Multiple Substitution*

The student replaces one element in the sentence with another and is consequently obliged to effect other changes.

#### 8.6.2a VERBS

This type of item can measure the student's control of a variety of verb forms, particularly those with spelling irregularities.

Here is a sample item in French:

Il mange du pain.   (nous)
Nous mangeons du pain.

#### 8.6.2b ADJECTIVES AND ARTICLES

Often a change of noun will require modification of the adjective or article.

Here are two sample items in German:

1. Wo ist der Hund?   (Katze)
   Wo ist die Katze?

2. Seine Mutter kam schnell.   (Vater)
   Sein Vater kam schnell.

In other cases the position of the adjective would change.

Here is a sample item in Spanish:

Este es un buen libro.   (español)
Este es un libro español.

### 8.6.2c PREPOSITIONS

In a language such as German, a change in the preposition may necessitate a modification of the complement.

Here is a sample item:

Fritz kommt mit seiner Schwester.  (ohne)
Fritz kommt ohne seine Schwester.

### 8.6.3 *Modified Substitution*

The student must modify the new element before substituting it in the sentence. In most European languages, verbs, adjectives, and occasionally nouns and adverbs possess different forms.

Here is a sample item in Spanish:

Juana se acostó.  (vestirse)
Juana se vistió.

Sometimes the change also necessitates a different word order.

Here is a sample item in German:

Er brachte die Butter.  (wegnehmen)
Er nahm die Butter weg.

### 8.6.4 *Replacement*

The student replaces a noun or phrase with the appropriate pronoun(s).

Here is a sample item in French:

Il donne le livre à Pierre.
Il le lui donne.

### 8.6.5 *Transformation*

The following transformations have proved effective as writing-test items.

### 8.6.5a NUMBER

Sentences may be changed from singular to plural or plural to singular.

Here is a sample item in French:

Le cheval est là-bas.  (plural)
Les chevaux sont là-bas.

### 8.6.5b WORD ORDER

Sentences may be changed to begin with the underlined word.

Here is a sample item in German:

Ich weiß nicht, wie sie es macht.
Wie sie es macht, weiß ich nicht.

### 8.6.5c TENSE

Sentences may be changed to a new tense. Many possible combinations exist.

Here is a sample item in Spanish:

Leía el libro si no tenía prisa.   (present)
Leo el libro si no tengo prisa.

### 8.6.5d VOICE

Sentences may be changed from the active to the passive voice or from the passive to the active.

Here is a sample item in German:

Man kauft diesen Tisch.   (passive)
Dieser Tisch wird gekauft.

### 8.6.5e MODE

Sentences may be changed from the subjunctive to the indicative mode or from the indicative to the subjunctive.

Here is a sample item in French:

Pierre va à Paris.   (il faut que)
Il faut que Pierre aille à Paris.

### 8.6.5f NEGATIVE

Sentences may be changed to the negative.

Here is a sample item in German:

Sie studiert zu Hause.   (nicht)
Sie studiert nicht zu Hause.

### 8.6.5g INTERROGATIVE

Sentences may be changed to the interrogative.

Here is a sample item in Spanish:

Pablo irá al concierto.   (interrogative)
¿Irá Pablo al concierto?

### 8.6.6 *Obeying Commands*

Items of this type test primarily word order and verb forms. Complex commands can necessitate changes in pronouns.

Here are two sample items in French:

1. Dites à Madame Lasalle de ne pas se lever.
   Ne vous levez pas, Madame.

2. Dites à Pierre qu'il vous rendra le journal ce soir.
   Tu me rendras le journal ce soir.

### 8.6.7 *Joining Sentences*

The student's ability to use conjunctions and relative pronouns, as well as his understanding of verb tenses, modes, and word order, can be evaluated with the following type of written test with printed cues. The student is given two independent statements and is asked to join them into one complex or compound sentence.

Here are some sample items in French.

#### 8.6.7a INDICATIVE CLAUSES

Je suis certain. Paul viendra à deux heures.
Je suis certain que Paul viendra à deux heures.

#### 8.6.7b SUBJUNCTIVE CLAUSES

Je suis content. Pierre va à l'école.
Je suis content que Pierre aille à l'école.

#### 8.6.7c CONJUNCTIONS WITH SUBJUNCTIVE

J'aide ma sœur. Elle peut finir son travail.   (pour que)
J'aide ma sœur pour qu'elle puisse finir son travail.

#### 8.6.7d CONJUNCTIONS WITH INDICATIVE

Nous n'y allons pas. Il fait trop froid.   (parce que)
Nous n'y allons pas parce qu'il fait trop froid.

Items of the four types given above could be mixed so that the student would have to choose between the indicative and the subjunctive. Such items are also very appropriate in Spanish.

#### 8.6.7e RELATIVE PRONOUNS

Cette dame est ma cousine. Elle passe là-bas.
Cette dame qui passe là-bas est ma cousine.

**8.6.8**  *Directed Questions and Answers*

Question-answer items, in which the proper response is suggested to the student, offer still another variation of the brief writing-test item that can be easily and objectively scored. The student is requested to supply either the answer or the question.

Question-answer items lend themselves equally well to oral and to written presentation. If only one element is to be tested, each item must be carefully checked to remove any words that would require an additional transformation. In other instances, it might prove valuable to examine several aspects of the language in the same item.

The following questions in French show how different elements can enter into the answers.

**8.6.8a**  NEGATIVE: WORD ORDER

Votre mère arrive-t-elle ce matin?   (non)
Non, elle n'arrive pas ce matin.

**8.6.8b**  NEGATIVE: PARTITIVE

Désirez-vous de l'eau?   (non, merci)
Non, merci, je ne désire pas d'eau.

**8.6.8c**  VERB FORMS

Lisez-vous ce roman?   (oui)
Oui, je lis ce roman.   (*or* Oui, nous lisons ce roman.)

**8.6.8d**  PRONOUNS

A-t-il écrit cette lettre à son frère?   (non)
Non, il ne la lui a pas écrite.

(Note: The item above tests pronoun forms, word order, and the agreement of the past participle.)

**8.6.8e**  PREPOSITIONS WITH PLACE NAMES

Où allez-vous cet été?   (Canada)
Je vais au Canada.   (*or* Nous allons au Canada.)

**8.6.8f**  QUESTIONS: INTERROGATIVE FORMS

The underlined word or words represent the response to the question to be formulated.

1. J'aime le livre bleu.
     Quel livre aimez-vous?

2. Marie a <u>cinq ans</u>.
   Quel âge a Marie?

3. J'écris avec <u>mon stylo</u>.
   Avec quoi écrivez-vous?

### 8.6.9   *Sentence Construction (Dehydrated Sentences)*

An effective writing test may be created by having the students construct a sentence from a selected group of nouns, pronouns, adjectives, verbs, and adverbs. Nouns and pronouns would be given in the nominative; verbs would appear in the infinitive form. Thus, a sample item in French would look like this:

Cue: hier / tante / aller / église
Response: Hier ma tante est allée à l'église.

In a more highly inflected language, such as German, this type of test permits effective examination of the students' grasp of a large variety of morphological forms.

Cue: gestern / groß / Mann / gehen / Stadt
Response: Gestern ist der große Mann in die Stadt gegangen.

It is also possible to furnish a model sentence and then provide a set of elements to be incorporated into a similar sentence. Here is a sample item in Spanish:

Model: Ha venido para que yo lo ayude.
Cue: llegar / sin que / tú / la / llamar
Response: Ha llegado sin que tú la llames.

Sentence-construction items constitute an excellent test for students of junior-high age or over. Most students enjoy the challenge such a test provides. Moreover, it reproduces the problems the student faces writing in the target language with the aid of a dictionary. From the examiner's point of view, such a test may be scored objectively, and the scores are reliable because it removes the stumbling block that traditional translation tests create for the students with poor vocabulary recall.

### 8.6.10   *Picture Writing*

With picture writing, directed-writing test items can be developed in which the student's performance will be measured independently of his listening and reading skills. In addition, the student will not have recourse to his native language. The system of ideograms has been briefly described in

Section 6.8.13. Once the student knows the symbols, he will be able to understand the ideogram easily; the test will then evaluate only his proficiency in writing.

Here are two sample items in English:

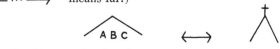

The school is far from here.

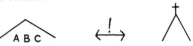

The hospital is three kilometers from here. (The symbol ✕ means here; ⟵ ··· ⟶ means far.)

The school is near the church.

The school is very near the church; ( ⟷ is near; ! means very).[1]

## 8.7 DIRECTED PASSAGES

Passage tests provide a continuity lacking in pattern-drill and sentence tests. The passage given to the student may be presented orally or in written form. Obviously, an oral presentation will confront the student with problems of listening comprehension and spelling that he will not have if the passage is printed.

### 8.7.1 *Passage Transposition: Change of Tenses*

A short narrative is read in its entirety. The same passage is then read again with pauses between sentences, and the student is asked to transpose the passage in time. For example, a passage may be read in the future and the student asked to rewrite it in the present tense. A more difficult test, and one in which it might be advisable to present the students with a written passage, requires the students to rewrite a selection in past time. In French, this would necessitate the student's distinguishing between the passé composé and the imperfect, as well as knowing the proper forms of those tenses. Spanish

---

[1] See *TAVOR Aids Bulletin*, No. 5 (May 1966), p. 2.

presents similar problems. In German, the problem of word order would appear in any passage being rewritten in a compound tense.

### 8.7.2   *Passage Transposition: Change of Style*

A dialogue is read, and the student is asked to retell the conversation in indirect discourse. The simplest form of such a test would have the principal verbs in the present tense.

In this type of test, too, the time element may be introduced. When the main verbs are placed in the past (for example, "Le dije que . . . ," "Jacques a dit que . . ."), the student is obliged to modify the tenses of the verbs in the subordinate clauses. In German, the student would be required to demonstrate his familiarity with the subjunctive and its uses.

A variation of this test has the teacher read the indirect version of the conversation. The students then reproduce the dialogue as it was actually spoken. Many students tend to find this test more difficult than the former.

### 8.7.3   *Retelling a Story*

The teacher reads a short story which the students must then retell in their own words. To minimize the element of recall and thus prevent favoring the students with better memory, the narrative could be accompanied with one or more pictures, illustrating the situation. Advanced students may be asked to relate the story in a different tense, or from a different point of view, or in a different literary style (that of a journalist, a detective-story author, a romance writer, etc.).

For scoring this type of test, the teacher would organize a system like the following:

1. accuracy of recall:                                               5  points
2. spelling:                                                         5  points
3. verb forms and tenses:                                          10  points
4. fluency of style
   (use of adverbs, conjunctions, clauses):  10  points
5. choice of vocabulary:                                          5  points

Of course, the objectives of a particular quiz or course unit would dictate the choice of aspects to be scored and the relative weight (that is, the number of points) assigned to each. Considerations such as 4 and 5 are important in encouraging students to develop sophistication in written expression. When scores are based only on content and grammatical accuracy, the student for whom grades are of greater value than experimentation will limit his essays to words he is totally sure of and will rely on the simplest structures.

### 8.7.4 *Writing a Dialogue*

The student receives a copy of a skeleton dialogue in which key words are indicated. He is asked to write out a complete conversation, using the key words logically.

Here is a brief sample item in English:

Joe: nice day!
Janet: walk?
Joe: where?
Janet: forest / flowers
Joe: fine

The student is graded on appropriate use of the key words, correctness of grammar and spelling, and natural expression.

## 8.8 VOCABULARY

The ability to write a foreign language presupposes a knowledge of the lexical units of the language. In this sense, a lexical unit is a word or group of words possessing a specific meaning. Just as one word can have different meanings in different contexts, so may that word represent several lexical units. Consider the following example in English:

Joe belongs to the human *race*.
Joe went to the dog *race*.
Joe and Sam *race* each other.
Joe and Sam *race* across the room and out the door.
Joe and Sam *race* their turtles.

The effective vocabulary test should be constructed around lexical units rather than words.

Written vocabulary tests evaluate the student's ability to recall and to produce lexical units in the new language. Vocabulary items may be developed for use in conjunction with visual, printed, or oral cues.

### 8.8.1 *Pictures*

Visual cues, while particularly effective in the elementary school, may be profitably used at all levels of instruction. If stick figures or simplified line drawings have been used in class, they may also be used in vocabulary tests. Pictures may be cut from magazines and mounted on cards. Care must be taken to avoid the possibility of an ambiguous interpretation of a picture; if necessary, scoring can be modified to allow a certain range of correct responses. The visual cue may also be accompanied by a written cue to focus student attention on the specific lexical unit to be furnished.

### 8.8.1a   NOUNS

Noun items can test elementary vocabulary as well as advanced technical vocabulary. The students must furnish a definite or indefinite article in the case of languages possessing gender. Both singular and plural forms can be tested.

Here is a sample item in French:

Cue:

Qu'est-ce que c'est?
Response: une maison (la maison *or* C'est une maison.)

Here is a sample item in Spanish:

Cue:

¿Qué ve Ud.?
Response: caballos (Veo dos caballos.)

### 8.8.1b   ADJECTIVES

Whereas certain common descriptive adjectives (such as the colors) may be easily identified through pictures alone, more complex items would combine pictures with an oral or written cue. This type of item permits the testing of adjective forms and their comparison.

Here is a sample item in German:

Cue: 

Hier ist ein _____ Hut und da liegt ein weißer Hut.
Response: schwarzer

Here is a sample item in French:

Cue: 

Jean est grand, mais sa mère est _____ que lui.
Response: plus grande

### 8.8.1c  VERBS

The more common verbs, especially the action verbs, lend themselves to picture tests.

Here is a sample item in Spanish:

Cue:

¿Qué hace?
Response: Duerme

The cue question can also be worded so that students must furnish the infinitive. For example: Qu'est-ce qu'il aime faire? Response: Courir.

### 8.8.1d  PREPOSITIONS

Pictures or diagrams may be used to define prepositions directly and unambiguously. If only the meaning of prepositions is to be tested, then a written cue should be included.

Here is a sample item in French:

Cue:

Le chapeau est _____ la chaise.
Response: sur

In an inflected language such as German, the same item could require the use of the appropriate article; in this case the gender of the word *chair* should be given unless everyone is totally familiar with the word. For example:

Cue: Da ist der Stuhl. Mein Hut ist _____ Stuhl.
Response: auf dem

Note: It is quite difficult to find or to sketch a picture that presents an unambiguous definition of a specific adverb. In many cases, as with adverbs of time, it is impossible.

### 8.8.2  *Series*

Students are asked to furnish the missing word in a common series.

Here are some sample items:

Cue: lundi, mardi, _____, jeudi
Response: mercredi

Cue: febrero, _____, abril
Response: marzo

Cue: achtzehn, neunzehn, _____
Response: zwanzig

### 8.8.3 *Numbers*

Students are asked to write out numbers, dates, and simple arithmetic operations.

Here is a sample item in Spanish:

Cue: $5 - 3 = 2$
Response: Cinco menos tres hacen dos.

### 8.8.4 *Synonyms*

Students are asked for a word or expression similar in meaning to the word given.

Here are some sample items in German and French:

Cue: Gewiß!
Response: Sicher!

Cue: Marie est contente.
Response: Marie est heureuse.

### 8.8.5 *Antonyms*

Students are asked to write the word or expression whose meaning is the opposite of the word given.

Here are sample items in Spanish and German:

Cue: oscuro
Response: claro

Cue: schwer
Response: leicht

Another variation of this type of item requires the students to give the opposite of the word or words underlined in a sentence.

Here is a sample item in French:

Cue: Sa tasse est vide.
Response: Sa tasse est pleine.

An item of the above sort could be scored 1 point for choice of word and 1 point for accuracy in spelling, adjective agreement, etc.

### 8.8.6 *Related Words*

As the students continue their language instruction, they learn to recognize related words. Vocabulary items can assess their ability to produce related forms.

#### 8.8.6a NOUNS

Give the related noun.

Here are some sample items in German:

Cue: dumm
Response: die Dummheit

Cue: pünktlich
Response: die Pünktlichkeit

#### 8.8.6b ADJECTIVES

Give the related adjective.

Here are some sample items in French:

Cue: salir
Response: sale

Cue: fausser
Response: faux

#### 8.8.6c VERBS

Give the related verb.

Here are some sample items in Spanish:

Cue: narración
Response: narrar

Cue: sonriente
Response: sonreír

### 8.8.7 *Definitions*

By defining lexical units the student shows his knowledge of vocabulary within the context of the foreign language.

#### 8.8.7a ONE LEXICAL UNIT

The student answers a question or fills in a blank.

Here are two sample items in French:

Cue: Qu'emploie-t-on pour couper la viande?
Response: un couteau

Cue: J'emploie mon couteau pour ——————— la viande.
Response: couper

### 8.8.7b  SIMPLE-SENTENCE CONSTRUCTION

Advanced students may be asked to write a sentence showing that they
are familiar with the meaning of a given lexical unit.

Here is a sample item in German:

Cue: klopfen
Response: Der Mann klopft an die Tür.

Items of this sort should be assigned 2 points: 1 for comprehension and
1 for accuracy of expression. The quiz as a whole could receive two scores
or grades.

### 8.8.7c  MULTIPLE-SENTENCE CONSTRUCTION

A variation of the above item (8.8.7b) requires students to use one word
or phrase in as many different lexical units as they can by constructing sentences in the target language.

Here is a sample item in French:

Cue: compte
Responses: Jean compte son argent.
　　　　　Marie compte venir ce soir.
　　　　　Il a écrit son compte rendu.
　　　　　Tout compte fait, il s'est bien amusé.

### 8.8.7d  WRITING DEFINITIONS

Advanced students who possess a certain command of the foreign language
can be asked to write definitions of lexical units in the target language. The
definitions of difficult words or phrases would be scored for both comprehension and accuracy of expression. The definitions of common lexical units
would be scored for both appropriateness or imagination and accuracy of
expression.

## 8.9 COMPOSITION

Whereas hybrid writing tests and dictations objectively measure the various writing skills, a composition measures the student's ability to organize his thoughts, to choose his vocabulary, to formulate his sentences—in short, to commit his ideas to paper.

Yet foreign-language composition tests, like English essay tests, have two drawbacks: scoring is time-consuming and grades tend to lack objectivity. Not only will different teachers assign different grades to the same paper, but a teacher reading a set of papers for a second time will rarely give them the same grades as he gave after the first reading. However, since composition is an art in which students—especially advanced language students—are expected to gain proficiency, composition tests cannot be ignored. Through careful advance preparation, the scoring of these tests can be simplified and their reliability increased.

### 8.9.1 *Planning the Test*

Realizing that a composition test calls upon various abilities, the teacher will determine one or perhaps two or three limited objectives for each test. Thus, rather than assigning an overall score based on a quick impression gained from a single reading, the teacher will grade only one (or two or three) aspects of the composition. Since the student's knowledge of certain patterns or verb forms can be measured more reliably and efficiently on other tests, the composition should be scored for aspects not covered by more objective quizzes. Certain types of objectives and appropriate subjects for test items are suggested in the following section.

### 8.9.2 *Vocabulary-Based Composition*

In a vocabulary-oriented composition, the main objective is to evaluate the richness and appropriateness of the student's recall or active vocabulary. To score this type of composition, the teacher could assign one grade for richness and another for appropriateness (that is, accurate choice of words). To simplify the scoring, these grades could be limited to three categories: poor, satisfactory, and good.

#### 8.9.2a USE OF NOUNS

Students are asked to describe a room, a street scene, a farmyard, a menu, or the like. Objectivity is greatly increased if all students are asked to describe a particular picture, perhaps a textbook illustration or a large picture hung at the front of the classroom.

### 8.9.2b USE OF ADJECTIVES AND ADVERBS

Students are asked to compare and contrast two similar pictures. Illustrations can be chosen that elicit number and color words or that require the comparative and superlative forms of adjectives and adverbs.

### 8.9.2c USE OF VERBS

Students are asked to narrate an experience: a day at school, a typical Sunday, a trip. To increase the reliability of the test, students may be asked to narrate the action suggested by a picture or a series of pictures. Subjects such as "Ce que Jean fait avant de se coucher" or "Ce que je fais avant de venir à l'école" encourage the use of common reflexive verbs in French.

## 8.9.3 *Grammar-Oriented Composition*

Students may be given a subject that requires them to use certain morphological structures.

### 8.9.3a PARTITIVE (IN FRENCH)

Students are asked to write a personal account of a festive meal or birthday dinner; they might describe the differences between a French *déjeuner* and an American lunch.

### 8.9.3b VERB TENSES

Students are asked to narrate, in the past, present, or future, the actions shown in a series of pictures. They might look at a cartoon strip and be asked to present the dialogue in indirect speech.

### 8.9.3c NECESSITY

To encourage use of words like *falloir* and *devoir, müssen* and *sollen, es necessario* and *deber,* select a topic that requests instructions and explanations: "Comment faut-il étudier le français?" or "¿Qué debemos hacer antes de hacer un viaje?" Such compositions could also be graded for vocabulary, if desired.

## 8.9.4 *"Point of View" Composition*

The "point of view" composition challenges the student's imagination and tests his consistency of style. The target language becomes a vehicle of individual expression. The possibilities are endless and can be adapted to all levels.

### 8.9.4a PHYSICAL DESCRIPTIONS

Descriptions may concern units studied in class. When students have finished a unit based on the house, they may be asked to describe a house as seen by a midget, or by the family dog, or by an American Indian of the past century.

### 8.9.4b EMOTIONAL STATES

Students are asked to describe a scene or situation as seen through the eyes of someone who is elated (or sad or extremely tired).

### 8.9.4c PERSONALITY

Students are asked to describe a scene or narrate an event in the style either of a specific onlooker—a grandmother, for example—or of two different observers, an old miser and a poor orphan, a teen-age girl and a grandmother, and so on.

### 8.9.5 *Letter-Writing Conventions*

Students are asked to write a business letter requesting a service or product, a thank-you note to a friend's mother, an invitation to a party. Letters are graded on the proper use of formulas as well as on overall tone.

### 8.9.6 *Thought-Provoking Essays* [1]

Composition topics should be precisely worded to make the grading as objective as possible. Subjects may be drawn from political events, school happenings, current controversies. Papers may be scored on logical reasoning, organization, sophistication, or effective communication. If language and expression comprise the primary points to be tested, the subject could be discussed in class orally and the written test given at the end of the period.

## 8.10 TRANSLATION

Thirty years ago almost all writing tests were translation tests. These took the form of paragraphs and sentences to be translated or incomplete sentences in the target language containing words to be translated. Such tests were relatively easy to prepare and lent themselves to efficient and fairly reliable scoring. More recently, both teachers and language specialists have begun to question the *validity* of such translation tests.

[1] Literature tests will be treated in Chapter 9.

Basically, the translation test hinges on a knowledge of vocabulary: if the student cannot recall the foreign-language equivalent of the English word, he obviously cannot demonstrate his ability to handle the structures of the language. Thus, in testing the language proficiency of beginners or intermediate students, the teacher obtains more valid results in testing vocabulary and structure separately.

### 8.10.1 *Vocabulary*

Many teachers employing audio-lingual methods prefer to use only the type of vocabulary items suggested earlier (see Section 8.8). The following vocabulary-translation tests do, however, merit consideration.

#### 8.10.1a WORD LISTS

Word-list tests are probably the *least* effective vocabulary tests because the knowledge of pairs of words reflects neither the ability of the student to retain these words nor, more important, the ability to use the words properly.

#### 8.10.1b WORDS IN CONTEXT: SPECIFIC LEXICAL UNITS

Adverbs, conjunctions, and idiomatic expressions lend themselves poorly to target-language definitions. Testing these items in context more accurately reflects the thinking processes of an intermediate or advanced student who can handle many patterns and lexical units freely in the new language but still has to look up words he has forgotten or has not yet learned.

Here are sample items in French and Spanish:

Jean is coming as soon as possible.
Jean vient _____ possible.

Correct response: aussitôt que

He's not tall, but short.
No es alto _____ bajo.

Correct response: sino

It is sounder linguistically to present the English sentence first and then the incomplete equivalent in the foreign language rather than mix an English word in parentheses with the target-language sentence. The student is able to grasp the entire idea in English before formulating the equivalent idea in the target language. Moreover, such items serve to reinforce the correct English–to–foreign-language correspondence between the other elements in the sentence.

### 8.10.1c WORDS IN CONTEXT: FALSE COGNATES

Items of the type shown above are also very effective in testing familiarity with the false cognates existing between two languages.

Here is a sample item in German:

He wants to become a soldier.
Er will Soldat _____.

Correct response: werden

### 8.10.1d WORDS IN CONTEXT: IRREGULAR DISTRIBUTION

Such items are useful in testing lexical units with unequal distribution in English and the target language. Sometimes one English word corresponds to two or more words in the target language and vice versa.

Here are two sample items in French:

Jeanne was rather sad, but tried to hide her feelings.
Jeanne était _____ triste, mais elle essayait de cacher ses sentiments.

Correct response: assez

I'd rather go to the movies than to the theater.
J'aimerais _____ aller au cinéma qu'au théâtre.

Correct response: mieux (*or* plutôt)

### 8.10.2 *Grammatical Structure*

Knowledge of grammar can also be measured through discrete translation items. Familiar vocabulary should be employed to avoid introducing two variables. Equivalent sentences in English and the target language help reinforce proper correspondences between the two languages. The translation may be made into English or into the target language.

Here are some sample items:

The lady you met is my mother.
Die Dame, _____, ist meine Mutter.

Correct response: die Sie getroffen haben

I wonder what time it is?
¿Qué hora _____?

Correct response: será

Quand tu viendras, apporte-moi un verre d'eau.
When you _____, bring me a glass of water.

Correct response: come

### 8.10.3 *Translation as an Art*

For advanced students, familiar with vocabulary and structure, the translation of a passage from English into the target language becomes a refined exercise in style. In this context, the translation test becomes both reliable and valid. Translation tests may be rendered more objective by isolating those structures or forms that present particular difficulty and by constructing items similar to those in Section 8.10.1c. Translations may be scored for accuracy (in a scientific article, for example) or for literary expression (in selections where tone and mood are of greater importance than a word-for-word rendering of the text).

# CHAPTER NINE
# CULTURE AND LITERATURE

Culture, as Edouard Herriot once defined it, is what is left when all has been forgotten: *"c'est ce qui reste quand on a tout oublié."* This phrase is useful in describing the cultured individual: if one long-range aim of the foreign-language teacher is to transmit to the student the target country's conception of the cultured man, then, paradoxically, he must actively teach those elements which the cultured man has forgotten—those elements which exist at the subconscious level.

Culture, in this broad sense, has two major components. One is anthropological or sociological culture: the attitudes, customs, and daily activities of a people, their ways of thinking, their frames of reference. Since language is a direct manifestation of this phase of culture, a society cannot be totally understood or appreciated without a knowledge of its language. The other component of culture is the history of civilization. Traditionally representing the "culture" element in foreign-language teaching, it includes geography, history, and achievements in the sciences, the social sciences, and the arts. These two phases of a particular society's culture are most closely joined in the literature that gives expression to that culture.

Literature is the written transcription of man's thoughts, feelings, and aspirations. While cultures or societies that do not have developed literatures exist, literature cannot come into being without culture. Fortunately many good features of a literary work survive translation; otherwise, few Americans, for example, could enjoy the Bible, the *Arabian Nights, War and Peace,* and Dante. Even so, the student who possesses a near-native command of Spanish has a marked advantage when reading Calderón over persons who must either rely on a translation or work slowly through the text, dictionary in hand. This student has the advantage because he can appreciate the *untranslatable:* both the tangible elements, such as the rhythm and flow and the precision of the author's expression, and the intangible—the intellectual and emotional response created by the tangible elements. The study of literature as an art and of the stylistic techniques of this art can only be approached through the language in which the literature was written.

## 9.1   TESTING CULTURE

### 9.1.1   *History of Civilization*

In the lower levels of audio-lingual instruction little time is devoted to the history of civilization. Students are encouraged, however, to do outside reading in English about subjects that interest them. Posters or reproductions of works of art may decorate the classroom walls. But the teacher generally has little time for formal instruction. Gone are the days of rote learning which saw test items like "Name five monuments to be found in Paris" or "List ten German scientists and their contributions." Today the subjects that comprise history of civilization are appropriately introduced in the readings, or they may be integrated into classroom activities. Geography, for example, may involve "buying" railroad tickets and "planning" voyages.

As the amount of reading increases in the upper levels, the students expand their knowledge of geography and history and develop an appreciation for the achievements of the target culture. Sometimes factual questions about the target culture are included in classroom tests.

In most cases, the student's factual knowledge of history of civilization is primarily measured by standard tests, such as the New York Regents, the College Boards, and the MLA Foreign Language Proficiency Tests for Teachers and Advanced Students.

The classroom teacher should be familiar with the types of items used on standardized tests even though he may not be developing similar tests for his own students. "Civilization" questions lend themselves nicely to the multiple-choice format. Let us look at the principal kinds of questions.

**9.1.1a**  IDENTIFICATION

All the following are capitals of South American countries *except*

A.  Lima.
B.  Bogotá.
C.  São Paulo.
D.  Caracas.

Correct response: C

**9.1.1b**  MATCHING

Each of the following French rulers is properly matched with the century of his reign *except*

A.  François I (16th century).
B.  Louis XIII (17th century).
C.  Napoleon I (18th century).
D.  Napoleon III (19th century).

Correct response: C

**9.1.1c**  DEFINITION

The German holiday of *Pfingsten* celebrates

A.  a religious feast.
B.  a famous battle.
C.  the peace treaty of the Thirty Years' War.
D.  the beginning of winter.

Correct response: A

**9.1.1d**  EXPLANATION

Which of the following explain why the Common Market was formed?

I.  The pooling of resources would make war between France and Germany materially impossible.
II.  The Common Market would promote closer economic ties among member nations.
III.  Gradually the member nations would set up common external tariffs on imports from non-members.

A.  I & II only
B.  I & III only
C.  II & III only
D.  I, II, & III

Correct response: D

### 9.1.2   *Cultural Differences between Peoples*

In the audio-lingual program of instruction the anthropological aspect of the target culture is introduced in the very first dialogues: the students learn how young people and adults greet each other, how they take leave of each other, how they carry out other everyday activities. From the beginning, the students notice differences between their own mode of life and that of the people whose language they are learning. Gradually they grow to appreciate the complexity of the concept of culture.[1]

Cultural differences may be of various sorts: What behavior and language patterns do the people of the target culture have? Why do they behave a certain way? What meaning is associated with a specific gesture or intonation or action? What are their daily habits and activities?

While students cannot actively participate in the target culture without traveling to the target country, they can learn about the living patterns of that country and simulate some of its conditions in the classroom. Tests employing some of the following item types will measure to what degree the student understands these cultural differences.[2]

#### 9.1.2a   TYPICAL VS. NON-TYPICAL

Mark the following statements as follows: A = | typical action or behavior |, B = | non-typical action or behavior |. (These examples are in English; for more advanced students the items may be in the target language.)

Here is a sample item for German:

For breakfast Herr Braun had orange juice, ham, and scrambled eggs.

Correct response: B

#### 9.1.2b   EXPLANATION

In each of the following cases select the most appropriate explanation for the action described.

Here is a sample item for French:

Dominique shouts: Hurray, it's Thursday!

    A. As usual there is no school.
    B. Only one more day of school till the weekend.
    C. School is out at two, rather than three, on Thursdays.

[1] A most useful sourcebook is Edward T. Hall's *The Silent Language* (New York: Doubleday, 1959). It is also available in a Fawcett paperback edition, R204.
[2] See Robert Lado, *Language Testing* (New York: McGraw-Hill, 1964), Part IV.

Correct response: A

### 9.1.2c TIME AND PLACE

Select the appropriate answer.

Here is a sample item for Spanish:

The Fonseca family in Madrid was at table when Enrique stopped by. He was surprised to find them eating, because it was

A. 12 noon.
B. 3 P.M.
C. 10 P.M.

Correct response: A

### 9.1.2d CONVERSATION

Select the appropriate phrase or rejoinder for a conversational situation.

Here is a sample item for French:

Alexis, age 10, is downtown and sees his teacher coming toward him. He extends his hand and says:

A. « Ça va? »
B. « Allô! »
C. « Bonjour, Monsieur ».

Correct response: C

## 9.2 TESTING LITERATURE

In this section we must draw a distinction between reading texts and literature. It is obvious that the student should be able to read the target language with a certain facility before undertaking a study of the literature. Facility is important; otherwise the study of a literary text is an exercise in decoding or deciphering. The student becomes engrossed in discovering what the author is saying without being able to analyze why or how it is said.

Often the reading skill is developed by having the student work with carefully selected short texts or excerpts.[1] At a more advanced level, longer literary works are read, and are read in their entirety. Yet at this point even novels will be treated primarily as vehicles for the development of vocabu-

---

[1] Consult the MLA Conference Newsletter: *Teaching Language Through Literature.* Published quarterly. Address correspondence to 501 Philosophy Hall, Columbia University, New York, N.Y. 10027.

lary, ease of expression (both oral and written), and direct comprehension of plot.

In this chapter we shall consider tests for advanced literature courses where the accent is on an appreciation of the artistic work and its background. This category includes Advanced Placement classes, survey of literature courses, and specialized courses organized by genre, period, or author.

### 9.2.1 *Objective Tests in Literature: Advantages and Limitations*

An objective-test item (whether a multiple-choice item or a direct question) is designed to elicit a specific response. The student's response, therefore, will be either clearly right or clearly wrong. The teacher can keep a record of the common wrong answers to certain questions and use them as distractors in multiple-choice items.

An objective test in literature *can* measure the following:

knowledge of chronology, authors, works, even content (plots, ideas, characters);

vocabulary: key words, their importance, their specific interpretation and use by the author;

ability to analyze specific features of a poem or a prose passage, to draw comparisons between works, periods, etc.

However, the objective test *cannot* measure:

accuracy and sophistication of student expression in the foreign language;

ability to interpret a literary selection;

ability to organize an essay, develop an introduction, choose related and salient examples, and draw a valid conclusion.

The question of literary interpretation is particularly delicate. Faced with several credible interpretations in a multiple-choice item, the student is prevented from searching for any other interpretation. In addition, the danger exists that the student will concentrate on discovering not the interpretation he finds most valid, but the interpretation he thinks the teacher most likely to have selected. On a particular item, either one interpretation is obviously correct and the three others are total misreadings of the text (the item is consequently relatively simple), or the choices are ambiguous, each containing an opinion that might be supported. It seems that a more reliable type of interpretation item could be developed, one containing the "interpretation" in the stem and requiring the student to select the best supporting quotation(s); however, such an item would tend to evaluate analysis and logical thinking rather than valid personal interpretation.

Test items for advanced students pose another problem. Literature courses of the type we are discussing are usually offered to fifth-year language students in high school or third-year language students in college. At this stage in their language education, students have become sophisticated objective-test takers. Thus, the teacher must take great care in the composition and selection of distractors.

### 9.2.2  *Essay Tests*

The limitations of the essay-type test must also be taken into account. First, there is the inequity of scoring. Those students who express themselves well and easily in the target language often obtain a high score even though their ideas are mediocre, while students who can give a more valid interpretation but possess less facility in the target language receive a lower grade. Some teachers, taking this phenomenon into account, occasionally give an essay test in English. Other teachers tell students that they may answer in the target language *or* in English, but that the highest possible grade for an English essay will be B+.

Second, many essay tests sample only a limited amount of the material that has been covered. Fortunately, a structured test can be developed in which the student is asked to introduce a greater amount of specific material.

Finally, essay tests are extremely difficult to score reliably. There is the ever-present tendency to expect good papers from good students and to make an *a priori* negative judgment about the work of the poor students. Some teachers admit that they grade by the "hunch" system: they have a "feeling" about how good a paper is. While an experienced teacher would probably not categorize a particular set of papers as "very good," "average," and "poor" on the first reading and then drastically revise these grades on a second reading a week later, the difference between a C+ and a B— is very hazy indeed, as it often is even between a C and a B. Two teachers reading the same set of papers will find that their scores vary even more sharply than those given by one teacher on two different occasions. In preparing a testing program for a literature class, the teacher must not forget these considerations.

### 9.3  LITERATURE TESTS: PLANNING

Usually very few tests are administered in a literature class. Therefore, many students study the types of tests and the content of the test items their teacher has given in the past in order to determine what material to learn. If the teacher planning a literature test has first reviewed the course objectives, such reviews can be helpful in orienting the students toward these objectives, which are generally divided into three areas: factual knowledge, textual comprehension, and individual expression. Each teacher determines the relative importance of the areas for each particular class.

### 9.3.1 *Knowledge*

Most literature teachers expect their students to have learned a certain number of facts. Some courses are built around facts about authors, works, characters, historical situations, and so on. Often students have to be able to identify quotations. Most teachers consider such knowledge as basic to any further discussion of the texts. They use factual tests or quizzes primarily to encourage a careful reading of major works and background material; since the tests are conceived primarily as "incentives," the grades scored on these tests, frequent in number though they may be, have little weight when the final grade is determined. Other teachers may consider the acquisition of factual knowledge a major objective of the course, rather than a step toward a major objective; in this case scores made on "knowledge" tests are an important factor in determining the student's final grade.

### 9.3.2 *Comprehension*

A primary objective, particularly in undergraduate literature classes, is comprehension. The course is so constructed that students will learn to read, analyze, and understand different types of texts. Both classwork and tests are built around series of questions designed to lead the student to pick out specific points, identify styles, determine themes and character development. The emphasis is on analysis, on the dissection of a literary work. On a test for such a class, the student usually identifies works and authors and answers questions on works studied in class or prepared outside of class, or even on an unfamiliar text.

### 9.3.3 *Expression*

There are two aspects to expression, both of which may be objectives of the literature class. One aspect is command of the target language: the acquisition of a literary vocabulary and an impersonal style. The second aspect is ability to synthesize or organize. Once the student has demonstrated his ability to examine a literary work, he must prepare an outline of his findings, and draw the relevant conclusions. Only a written essay test will enable the student to demonstrate his organizational ability. At its best, this type of test presents the student with a new idea or thesis that he is to criticize and interpret in the light of the course material.

**9.3.4**  *The Teacher's Schematic Outline*

In order to see how a literature test may be scored, let us take as an example the first-semester midterm examination of a French literature survey course. Generally the teacher assigns the following percentages to the objectives:

knowledge:        20 per cent
comprehension:  30 per cent
expression:        50 per cent

The expression part of the examination will be an essay question. Knowledge of the subject matter and comprehension will be tested by objective multiple-choice items.

The multiple-choice items will also be planned so that the course material is covered and so that the number of questions per subject will more or less correspond to the importance given that particular subject in the course. The teacher makes the following brief outline (subject to revision as he prepares the test) :

The multiple-choice section will include 50 questions: 20 to determine the students' knowledge of authors, themes, works, plot, etc., and 30 to assess their comprehension, that is, their ability to analyze a poem, to analyze a prose passage, and to draw comparisons between works and passages. 5 questions will treat the literary terms studied, and, since more study was given to the Middle Ages than to any other period, 27 questions will concern the Middle Ages; 18 will cover the Renaissance.

With this outline in mind, the teacher draws up the chart on page 172. As the multiple-choice items are prepared, he classifies each item according to the prior specifications. If necessary, the chart may be somewhat modified as the construction of the test progresses. The chart permits a certain degree of flexibility of choice as the items (indicated by tallies) are being written.

## 9.4   LITERATURE TESTS: CONSTRUCTING
## MULTIPLE-CHOICE ITEMS

The preparation of a multiple-choice section for a literature test is an especially challenging (and time-consuming) enterprise. The teacher who enjoys precise logical exercise and who does not become easily discouraged when the item analysis shows that certain items have furnished poor results (ambiguous? too difficult? too easy? more than one possible answer?) will appreciate the stimulation the preparation of such tests provides.

If possible, the teacher should prepare the outline chart for the examination well in advance. Throughout the course, he will note the material that

| OBJECTIVES / CONTENT | authors and characters | works and times | content:ideas and plot | content:themes | analysis of a poem | analysis of prose | drawing comparisons between passages | TOTALS |
|---|---|---|---|---|---|---|---|---|
| | KNOWLEDGE | | | | COMPREHENSION | | | TOTALS |
| **Middle Ages** | | | | | | | | |
| literary terms | | | | | ‖‖‖ | | | 5 |
| background | | // | | | | | | 2 |
| chansons de geste | | / | | | | / | // | 4 |
| Tristan | | | /// | | | /// | /// | 9 |
| littérature courtoise | / | | | / | | | | 2 |
| littérature bourgeoise | / | | / | | | | / | 3 |
| poésie | / | // | / | // | | / | / | 8 |
| **Renaissance** | | | | | | | | |
| background | / | | | | | | | 1 |
| Rabelais | | | / | | | / | // | 4 |
| La Pléiade | | / | | / | ‖‖‖ | | / | 8 |
| Montaigne | / | | | | | //// | | 5 |
| **TOTALS** | 5 | 5 | 5 | 5 | 10 | 10 | 10 | 50 |

Fig. 22

might be useful for future test items. Items from past examinations should be filed; often a good item can be modified and used on a later examination. The writing and editing of the test must be completed a week or so in advance of the examination date so that the items can be typed up and duplicated. During the pressure of examination time, a set of such papers can be scored and graded very quickly.

### 9.4.1 *Knowledge Items*

Knowledge items, often of the identification type, are the easiest to write and tend to prove quite reliable statistically. The advantage of the multiple-choice item over the simple question with written answer is twofold. First, students can answer a greater number of them within a given period of time; thus, the grade for that particular exam is based on a broader sampling of the subject matter. Second, the multiple-choice examination, even though more time-consuming to prepare, can be scored very rapidly. Third, it exclusively examines knowledge; a student's command of writing in the foreign language plays no role in the test. Moreover, the teacher is freed from the necessity to correct the inevitable errors of vocabulary and grammar.

The sample items in this section are taken from a French literature test.

#### 9.4.1a  AUTHORS

The student is asked to describe a writer or to identify the author of a quoted passage.

Lequel des écrivains suivants n'est *pas* un « chroniqueur » ?

A. Agrippa d'Aubigné
B. Philippe de Commynes
C. Geoffroy de Villehardouin
D. Jean de Joinville

Correct response: A

#### 9.4.1b  WORKS

Le sonnet « Heureux qui, comme Ulysse... » a paru dans quel recueil?

A. *Antiquités de Rome*
B. *Hymnes*
C. *Regrets*
D. *Elégies*

Correct response: C

In other items concerning works, the student may be asked to identify the work in which a particular quoted passage is found.

### 9.4.1c PLOT AND CHARACTER

Le gant comme symbole apparaît dans quel chapitre de *Tristan?*

    A. « L'Ermite Ogrin »
    B. « Brangien livrée aux serfs »
    C. « Le Jugement par le fer rouge »
    D. « La Forêt de Morois »

Correct response: D

### 9.4.1d THEMES

La question *ubi sunt* paraît dans un poème de du Bellay « Las! où est maintenant ce mépris de Fortune? » où le poète se plaint

    A. de la disparition de l'inspiration poétique.
    B. du manque de richesses.
    C. de l'éloignement de ses amis.
    D. du mépris des gens de Rome.

Correct response: A

### 9.4.2 *Comprehension Items*

Comprehension items are much more difficult to write and should be analyzed statistically whenever possible. Often the test situation will reveal a second valid response or some other kind of ambiguity; in this case the answer grid should be modified to allow the student credit for having selected either of the two possible responses. (Some teachers prefer to measure only knowledge with multiple-choice tests and to measure comprehension with a series of written questions and answers.)

### 9.4.2a LITERARY ANALYSIS

A short literary selection is followed by a series of multiple-choice items that test the student's analytical ability. Here, for example, is a sample selection from the poetry part of the French literature survey midterm examination.

> France, mère des arts, des armes et des lois,
> Tu m'as nourri longtemps du lait de ta mamelle;
> Ores, comme un agneau qui sa nourrice appelle,
> Je remplis de ton nom les antres et les bois.
>
> Si tu m'as pour enfant avoué quelquefois,
> Que ne me réponds-tu maintenant, ô cruelle?
> France, France, réponds à ma triste querelle!
> Mais nul, sinon Echo, ne répond à ma voix.

Entre les loups cruels j'erre parmi la plaine,
Je sens venir l'hiver, de qui la froide haleine
D'une tremblante horreur fait hérisser ma peau.

Las! tes autres agneaux n'ont faute de pâture,
Ils ne craignent le loup, le vent, ni la froidure:
Si ne suis-je pourtant le pire du troupeau!
Joachim du Bellay, Les Regrets

1. Ce poème est un(e)

  A. sonnet
  B. rondeau
  C. ode
  D. élégie

Correct response: A

If such an item is too simple for the level of the class, it may be modified so that instead of a recognition question it becomes in part a recall question. In the two sample items below and in Item 2, the student must remember the word "sonnet" and the characteristics of a sonnet in order to select the correct responses. Two modifications are possible: options may be presented with the initial and terminal letters or with only the initial letters.

Ce poème a la forme d'un(e)

  A. s_____t.     A. é
  B. r_____u.     B. o
  C. o__e.           C. r
  D. é_____e.     D. s

In the second case, above, it is desirable to arrange the options in alphabetical order.

2. Les rimes des deux premières strophes sont des rimes

  A. croisées.
  B. plates.
  C. embrassées.
  D. riches.

Correct response: C

Below we see how this item, too, may be transformed into a partial-recall question by using first and last letters or first letters only:

Dans les deux premières strophes le poète emploie une rime

A. c_____é.      A. c
B. e_____é.    B. e
C. p_____e.         C. p
D. r_____e.         D. r

3. Pour exprimer la détresse de l'exil, le poète s'identifie avec

A. la France, sa nourrice.
B. un agneau égaré.
C. le pire du troupeau.
D. les loups cruels.

Correct response: B

Such an item, which is relatively easy, tests whether the students have understood the major imagery of the poem.

4. Dans le vers quatorze, le poète met l'accent sur son

A. propre génie.
B. insuffisance.
C. besoin d'amitié.
D. amour pour la France.

Correct response: A

This item, built on the critical reading of one line, is much more difficult than Item 3, above.

5. Dans la dernière strophe le poète introduit l'idée de

A. la solitude.
B. l'injustice de son sort.
C. l'unité du troupeau.
D. la tristesse de la séparation.

Correct response: B

This question is similar to Item 4; it evaluates the student's critical reading of a part of the poem. While all four ideas expressed in the options are found in the poem, only B does not appear until the final verse.

6. Quel vers est particulièrement lent?

A. 2
B. 6
C. 7
D. 13

Correct response: C

This item evaluates student appreciation of rhythm and movement.

Short prose passages may also be presented in a multiple-choice format. Reading questions based on prose passages are often difficult to prepare since paragraph analysis is open to diverse interpretations; reading items based on poetry are easier to compose since most languages have some formal rules of versification.

### 9.4.2b  DRAWING COMPARISONS

Good comparison items can constitute an effective test, for the student is compelled to think about what he has read in order to arrive at valid conclusions.

Here is a sample item in French:

Si l'on juge l'amour de Tristan selon les idées de l'« art de vivre » de Montaigne, on critiquera surtout

A. l'adultère.
B. les souffrances des amants.
C. la volupté de leur amour.
D. les excès de la passion.

Correct response: D

Comparison items may be presented in conjunction with literary-analysis items. In this case, the passage or poem may lead to such questions as:

The main theme of the passage is similar to that of . . .
or:
Rabelais' ideas on education are

A. identical with those expressed in the passage.
B. in total contrast to those expressed in the passage.
C. etc.

## 9.5  LITERATURE TESTS: ESSAY QUESTIONS

In many literature classes, especially the more advanced ones, examinations are usually written tests often consisting of one or several essay questions. Since these classes are usually relatively small, the time saved scoring a multiple-choice test is often a consideration of minor importance. Unfortunately the written tests given in many literature classes are hastily prepared and of dubious validity and reliability.

### 9.5.1  *Essay-Test Reliability*

The reliability of an essay test tends to be limited by several factors: the language used (target or English), the length of the test, the vagueness of the subject, and non-comparative scoring.

#### 9.5.1a  LANGUAGE OF TEST

Literature tests given in the foreign language unfortunately have the effect of favoring those students who possess the most fluency in the language. (While it is admitted that literature classes should best be offered only to students whose command of the language presents no barrier either to understanding or to expression, it is true that this is frequently not the case. In graduate school libraries, English translations of French works are often checked out by the French majors, of German works by the German majors, and so on.) If fluency in the language constitutes one of the aims of the course, then it should, of course, be tested. But if other objectives are also considered important, it is advisable at least once a semester to assign a paper or examination in the students' native language so that the content alone will be judged.

#### 9.5.1b  LENGTH OF TEST

Within an hour, within even two or three, only a certain amount can be written by hand. Occasionally, teachers who feel that their examination insufficiently samples the material covered in class add an extra item or broaden existing questions at the last minute. The result is that many students are unable to finish the test within the allotted time, and the teacher —now feeling guilty about the length of the examination—debates whether to score the unfinished section zero or give it some credit.

The teacher can avoid this problem by choosing an essay topic whose scope can be covered within the allotted time. Not only does reliability in scoring increase—the speed factor is eliminated—but the students experience the satisfaction of handling the test question in a thoughtful, leisurely fashion. A set of multiple-choice questions or a series of short-answer questions, could be added to examine those subjects not included in the essay.

#### 9.5.1c  VAGUENESS OF SUBJECT

Many times the essay subject is poorly defined. The students receive the impression—perhaps correct—that the teacher just thought up a topic on the way to class.

Here, for example, is a subject which is too broad:

Discuss seventeenth-century French tragedy.

Since each student may select different aspects to write about, there will be little common ground on which to base the scoring. Often this lack of focus can be corrected if the teacher spends sufficient time before the examination selecting the specific points he wishes to have covered in the essay. An improved question might read:

> Explain the rules governing French classical tragedy and show their application in one of the plays you have read.

or:

> Compare and contrast *Andromaque* and *Le Cid*, considering dramatic structure and each author's conception of tragedy.

In the latter questions, since specific information is asked for, the teacher can outline a more reliable scoring system.

### 9.5.1d NON-COMPARATIVE SCORING

Often the teacher will read one student's test in its entirety, assign a grade, read the next student's test, and so on. This type of scoring has the effect of reinforcing the teacher's prior judgments: the good student's paper is automatically considered very good, the average student's paper as consistently average. Let us consider a more equitable method.

When scoring a set of fairly long examinations, the teacher can read just the first question on each examination and then place that paper in one of three or four piles according to the merit of the specific essay. When all have been classified, the teacher peruses one group at a time, assigning the grades with + or − according to relative merit. Then the papers are scrambled and the second question is read. Again the papers are grouped according to merit. Since the teacher is concentrating on only one question at a time, he can more reliably and objectively compare the performance of the various students.

### 9.5.2 *Essay-Test Validity*

Essay-test validity depends on the test's relevance to the course objectives. All tests measure something; the teacher must determine whether the essay test given is actually measuring the type of performance that corresponds to the intended objectives of the course.

### 9.5.2a KNOWLEDGE QUESTIONS: CLASS DISCUSSION

Frequently essay questions in literature courses are based on subject matter discussed in class. Let us look at the following question:

> Describe the polemic struggle of the Jesuits and the Jansenists in the mid-seventeenth century and define Pascal's role.

While based on a literary work, it does not actually require the student to have read Pascal. Many students do well on such a question simply by studying their class notes. If the course objective is teaching *about* French literature, such a question is valid. But if the course objective is to have the students read and appreciate the texts, then such a question must be regarded as one of dubious validity.

Let us look at another question:

Describe the originality of Giraudoux's theatrical works.

This question, when given to a class of advanced students who have studied drama at length, would be a thought question. Too often, however, a question like this appears on a test in a survey of literature class or in a twentieth-century literature class. The students have probably read only one play by Giraudoux and very few plays from other periods. They will only be able to repeat what they have read about the playwright's originality or what they have heard the teacher mention in class.

### 9.5.2b   KNOWLEDGE QUESTIONS: READING

To encourage careful reading of the texts, many teachers ask identification questions. Here are some examples:

Identify the following characters and briefly describe their roles.

Identify the following quotations and situate them in the work as a whole.

As long as the passages cited are representative of the author's style and thought, such questions are valid tests of the students' familiarity with the texts.

### 9.5.2c   THOUGHT QUESTIONS

As we have seen, many questions, purporting to be thought questions, are really knowledge questions. The valid thought question presents the student with a problem, an interpretation, a comparison, which has *not* been mentioned in class. At the same time, the problem is carefully defined so that, within the limits of his knowledge and his reading and within the time limitations of the test, the student can handle it satisfactorily.

Let us look at some possible thought questions.

Too broad:

Discuss the problem of liberty as it presents itself to Roland, Tristan, Rodrigue, and Oreste.

Discuss the theme of love in *Tristan et Iseut*, *Le Cid*, and *Andromaque*.

Within an hour the student cannot even begin to define "liberty" (in the first question), much less do an adequate job in relating the conception to four diverse protagonists. The definition of "theme" and "love" (in the second question) is also complex. The danger of such topics is that they encourage gross oversimplification on the part of the students.

Properly limited:

Roland, Tristan, Rodrigue, and Oreste are not entirely free in their actions. Compare and contrast the factors which influence the decisions made by these protagonists.

Describe the type of love presented in *Tristan et Iseut, Le Cid,* and *Andromaque.* What role does love play in each of these works?

It is also reasonable to offer the students some choice in their treatment of a subject: they may choose two (or three) out of four protagonists or two out of three works.

In another version of the thought question, the students are presented with a quotation or a new idea which they must apply to what they have read:

Baudelaire was impressed by Poe's classification of poetry as either descriptive or evocative. Apply Poe's distinction to the work of three poets we have studied this semester.

The carefully prepared essay question provides a challenging finish to a well-taught advanced literature class.

# APPENDIX
# COMMERCIAL
# LANGUAGE TESTS

Commercial language tests may be classified under four headings: prognostic tests, progress tests (to accompany a specific set of instruction materials), achievement tests, and proficiency tests. While the following list in no way pretends to be complete, it does include descriptions of the most widely used tests.[1]

## A.1 PROGNOSTIC TESTS

**A.1.1** *Carroll-Sapon Modern Language Aptitude Test* (MLAT) (The Psychological Corporation, 304 East 45th Street, New York, N.Y. 10017), 1959.

Age group: English-speaking persons, 9th graders to adults. (An elementary version of the MLAT is now in preparation.)

Forms: two

Administration: by school

Tape: yes (not needed for the Short Form)

Length: 60–70 minutes (Short Form without Parts I and II—30 minutes)

[1] Consult Oscar K. Buros, *Mental Measurements Yearbook* (Highland Park, N.J.: Gryphon Press, 1938, 1941, 1949, 1953, 1959, 1965), for reviews of current foreign-language tests; and see his *Tests in Print* (Gryphon Press, 1961).

Description: The test has five parts:

Part I: Number Learning. Students learn numbers in a new language. This part measures auditory memory and auditory alertness (tape).

Part II: Phonetic Script. Students learn phonetic script and select the correct transcription for words spoken on the tape. This part measures sound-symbol association ability (tape).

Part III: Spelling Clues. Students select the correct meaning of coded English words (a high-speed section). This part measures English vocabulary and, to some extent, sound-symbol association.

Part IV: Words in Sentences. Students handle diverse aspects of grammar in English, without using specific terminology. This part measures sensitivity to grammatical structure.

Part V: Paired Associates. Students memorize pairs of words. This part measures ability to learn rapidly by rote.

**A.1.2** *Pimsleur Language Aptitude Battery* (Harcourt, Brace & World, Inc., 757 Third Avenue, New York, N.Y. 10017), 1966.

Age group: English-speaking students in grades 6–12
Tape: yes
Length: 50–60 minutes
Administration: by school
Description: The test has six parts:

Part I: Grade-Point Average. Using a four-point scale, the students indicate the grades they last received in English, social studies, mathematics, and science.

Part II: Interest. Using a five-point scale, students evaluate their interest in studying foreign languages.

Part III: Vocabulary. Students select synonyms for twenty-four English words.

Part IV: Language Analysis. Presented with a limited number of words and phrases in an unfamiliar language, the students are asked to select the foreign-language equivalents of various English sentences. This part measures ability to draw appropriate analogies and to reason logically using foreign-language materials.

Part V: Sound Discrimination. Students learn to discriminate orally between similar sounds in a new language. This part measures the ability to learn new phonemic distinctions and to recognize them in different contexts.

Part VI: Sound-Symbol Association. From groups of four similarly spelled nonsense words, students select the ones that agree with the sounds heard on tape. This part measures ability to associate English-language sounds with their written symbols.

## A.2  PROGRESS TESTS

Progress tests are designed to accompany a specific set of instructional materials. Most of the major publishers are now producing tests to accompany their language textbooks. The teacher is advised to request a copy of the commercial test and study it in the light of his own course objectives. Only then can he decide whether or not to order such tests for his classes.

## A.3  ACHIEVEMENT TESTS

**A.3.1** *Common Concepts Foreign Language Test* (California Test Bureau, Del Monte Research Park, Monterey, Calif., 93940), 1962.

Languages: French, German, Spanish (and English)
Levels: One (all grades)
Forms: two
Administration: by school
Skills tested: listening
Tape: yes
Length: 40 minutes
Description: The student hears sentences in the foreign language. He indicates his understanding of what he has heard by selecting from sets of four colored pictures the ones that have been correctly described.

**A.3.2** *MLA Cooperative Foreign Language Tests* (Educational Testing Service, Princeton, N.J. 08540), 1963.

Languages: French, German, Italian, Russian, Spanish
Levels: L (One–Two) and M (Three–Four)
Forms: two
Administration: by school
Skills tested: listening, speaking, reading, writing
Tape: yes
Length: listening—25 minutes; speaking—10 minutes; reading—35 minutes; writing—35 minutes
Description:
Listening. The first few items of the Level L test use pictures. Thereafter the student selects from the printed selections in his answer booklet the

correct rejoinders or correct answers to taped questions. The following
types of items are used: discrete statements or questions, questions about a
recorded conversation, appropriate rejoinders for a telephone conversation,
and, in Level M, questions about a longer recorded passage. The tests do
not measure listening comprehension independently of reading.

Speaking. Item types involve repetition of recorded sentences, reading
aloud, answering questions about pictures, and free oral description of a
picture.

Reading. The types of items include fill-in-the-blanks, substitution of words
or phrases, and questions on short reading passages. The entire test is
multiple-choice.

Writing. The items differ somewhat from language to language. In general
the following types are used: fill-in-the-blanks, transformation of sentences
(to the past, to the plural, etc.), dehydrated sentences, and directed composition.

**A.3.3** *Pimsleur Modern Foreign-Language Proficiency Tests* (Harcourt,
Brace & World, Inc., 757 Third Avenue, New York, N.Y. 10017), 1967.

Languages: French, German, Spanish
Levels: One and Two
Forms: one
Administration: by school
Skills tested: listening, speaking, reading, writing
Tape: yes
Length: listening—20 minutes; speaking—20 minutes; reading—35 min-
utes; writing—35 minutes
Description:

Listening. Part I contains 20 phonemic-accuracy items in the form of complete sentences. In Part II the student selects the most appropriate response to a spoken stimulus from among four printed responses. This test
may be used only for classes with reading skill.

Speaking. In Part I the student identifies objects pictured in the test booklet.
In Part II the student hears a number of sentences on tape and then reads
them aloud. In Part III the student responds orally to questions presented
on tape.

Reading. All the reading-comprehension items are based on short passages.
The entire test is multiple-choice.

Writing. The types of items vary somewhat from language to language. At
both test levels, however, there is a progression from fill-in-the-blank items
to controlled sentences (transformation and substitution) to free composition based on pictures.

**A.3.4** *Regents High School Examinations* (The State University of New York, The New York State Education Department, Albany, N.Y. 12224), revised annually.[1]

Languages: French, German, Hebrew, Italian, Spanish
Level: Three
Forms: one
Administration: on specified dates in the state of New York
Skills tested: listening, reading, writing
Tape: no (teacher reads script)
Length: three hours
Description: A typical examination has six parts:

Part I: Listening Comprehension. Students hear short paragraphs and select the correct answers to questions printed in their test booklets; reading skill is necessary.

Part II: Listening and Writing. Students write answers to oral questions.

Part III: Reading Comprehension. Students answer multiple-choice questions based on printed paragraphs.

Part IV: Culture. Students answer multiple-choice items testing knowledge of geography, history, art, literature, etc.

Part V: Completion. Students answer multiple-choice testing of grammar and vocabulary.

Part VI: Directed Composition. Students write an essay based on a brief outline given in English.

**A.3.5** *Affiliation Testing Program Language Tests* (ATP) (Catholic University of America, Washington, D.C. 20017), revised annually.

Languages: French, German, Spanish
Levels: Two
Forms: one
Administration: by school (prepared for Catholic schools)
Skills tested: listening, reading
Tape: no (teacher reads script)
Length: 90 minutes
Description: A typical examination measures the five aspects outlined below:

Listening Comprehension. The teacher reads a passage aloud, then asks questions; students select the correct responses from multiple-choice answers given in their test booklets. The teacher reads aloud discrete items or in-

[1] Retired forms of Regents examinations are reprinted and sold by Amsco School Publications Inc., Box 351, Cooper Station, New York, N.Y. 10003.

complete statements, and the students select the proper responses from the choices printed in their test booklets. The reading skill is necessary.

Grammar. Multiple-choice reading items test usage, structure, and particularly verb forms.

Vocabulary. French: discrete items test vocabulary in context and knowledge of synonyms and antonyms. Spanish: multiple-choice translation items.

Reading Comprehension. Multiple-choice questions based on printed passages.

Cultural Background. Multiple-choice questions about history, geography, literature, etc.

**A.3.6**   *AATG German Tests* (Adolph Wegener, Secretary-Treasurer, American Association of Teachers of German, Muhlenberg College, Box 43, Allentown, Pa. 18104).

Language: German
Levels: Two, Four
Forms: one
Administration: by school
Skills tested: reading
Tape: no
Length: 45 minutes
Description: For both levels, these are multiple-choice reading tests.

Part I: Vocabulary in Context.

Part II: Usage. The items are the multiple-choice, fill-in-the-blank type.

Part III: Reading Comprehension. Students read passages and answer questions (the higher level requires spot translations of words and phrases).

**A.3.7**   *Cooperative French Listening Comprehension Test* (Educational Testing Service, Princeton, N.J. 08540), 1955.

Language: French
Levels: Two through Five (one test)
Forms: two
Administration: by school
Skills tested: listening (but reading skill is necessary)
Tape: yes
Length: 30 minutes
Description: The test has four sections:

Phonemic Description (or phonemic accuracy). The student hears a sentence and selects the corresponding sentence from five printed options.

Answering Questions. The student hears a question and selects the appropriate response from five printed options.

Completion of Statements. The student hears a partial statement and selects the appropriate completion from five printed options.

Comprehension of Passages. The student hears a passage, then related questions, and he selects the appropriate response from five options.

**A.3.8** *College Board Achievement Tests* (Educational Testing Service, Princeton, N.J. 08540), revised annually.

Languages: French, German, Hebrew, Russian, Spanish
Levels: Two through Five (one test)
Forms: varied
Administration: in specified centers on dates announced in advance
Skills tested: reading
Tape: no
Length: 60 minutes
Description: Since the College Board Achievement Tests are written by rotating committees of professors, the format and item types may vary somewhat from year to year. All items are multiple-choice reading items. Typically such tests include the following item types: [1]

Situation Questions. This printed test measures familiarity with the spoken language. The student selects the appropriate statement from four or five options.

Usage Questions. This part includes substitution and fill-in-the-blank items, occasionally with English cues, and completion sentences.

Vocabulary Questions. This part includes discrete items that usually test vocabulary in context in the target language.

Reading-Comprehension Items. Passages are given, followed by questions on content and items on particular words and phrases, sometimes requesting the most appropriate English equivalents.

**A.3.9** *College Board Supplementary Achievement Tests* (Educational Testing Service, Princeton, N.J. 08540), revised annually.[2]

Languages: French, German, Italian, Russian, Spanish
Levels: Two through Five (one test)
Forms: varied
Administration: annually, on a specified date
Skills tested: reading (Italian), writing (Italian), listening (French, German, Italian, Russian, Spanish)

[1] In May 1968, a composite test will be given for the first time: 40 minutes—reading and structure; 20 minutes—listening. Thereafter this composite language test will be administered twice annually.
[2] When the composite test (see above) is introduced, supplementary listening tests will no longer be given.

Tape: yes

Length: Italian Achievement Test (reading and writing)—90 minutes; Listening-Comprehension Tests—30 minutes

Description:

Italian Achievement Test. This test is similar to the College Board Achievement Tests in other languages (see A.3.8) but includes a final section that measures student proficiency in writing.

Listening-Comprehension Tests. The types of items include short conversations followed by oral questions and printed responses, short questions with printed responses, long passages with oral questions and printed responses.

## A.4  PROFICIENCY TESTS

**A.4.1**  *College Board Advanced Placement Tests* (Educational Testing Service, Princeton, N.J. 08540), prepared annually.

Languages: French, German, Spanish

Level: Five

Forms: one

Administration: annually, on a specified date

Skills tested: listening, reading, writing

Tape: yes

Length: three hours

Description: These tests are administered to high-school seniors who have followed a specialized course of language study. The specific works of literature to be covered are announced at the beginning of each school year. Recent tests have included a section that measures listening comprehension (oral questions with printed responses) and sections that test note-taking (a recorded lecture), reading-comprehension (passage items), and textual compositions on literary topics.[1]

**A.4.2**  *College Board Achievement Tests* and *Supplementary Achievement Tests* (see A.3.8 and A.3.9).

Schools may buy retired copies of these tests for local administration as placement tests.

---

[1] For sample copies of the tests and a brief discussion of them, consult *German Quarterly* Vol. XXXVIII (September 1965), pp. 415–528. See also *French Review*, Vol. XXXIX (December 1965), pp. 439–56.

**A.4.3** *Graduate Record Examinations* (Educational Testing Service, Princeton, N.J. 08540), prepared annually.

Languages: French, Spanish
Level: candidates for graduate study
Forms: one
Administration: in specified centers on specified dates
Skills tested: reading
Tape: no
Length: three hours
Description: The Advanced French Test and the Advanced Spanish Test use reading-comprehension items to examine knowledge of literature and general familiarity with culture and civilization. These items also test vocabulary and grammar as well as sensitivity to style and the ability to follow the development of an author's thoughts.

**A.4.4** *MLA Proficiency Tests for Teachers and Advanced Students* (Educational Testing Service, Princeton, N.J. 08540), 1961.

Languages: French, German, Italian, Russian, Spanish
Level: present and prospective teachers
Forms: three
Administration: in specified centers on dates announced in advance
Skills tested: listening, speaking, reading, writing
Tape: yes (listening and speaking)
Length: listening—20 minutes; speaking—15 minutes; reading—40 minutes; writing—45 minutes; applied linguistics—40 minutes; civilization and culture—30 minutes; professional preparation—45 minutes.
Description: These tests are administered in three different combinations: (1) all seven tests, (2) the four skills tests, or (3) the three tests on linguistics, culture, and professional preparation. The professional-preparation test is in English and is the same for all five languages.

These tests are currently undergoing revision; descriptive material regarding present forms may be obtained from the Educational Testing Service and from the MLA.[1]

**A.4.5** *Graduate School Foreign Language Tests* (Educational Testing Service, Princeton, N.J. 08540), 1963–64.

Languages: French, German, Russian
Forms: one

[1] See also Wilmarth H. Starr, "MLA Foreign Language Proficiency Tests for Teachers and Advanced Students," *PMLA*, Vol. LXXVII (September 1962), pp. 31–42.

Administration: four times a year at participating graduate schools

Skills tested: reading

Tape: no

Length: two versions—80 and 100 minutes

Description: These tests are designed to evaluate the foreign-language reading proficiency of graduate-level degree candidates. Part I tests control of structure through both discrete items and passage items, all in the target language. Part II presents reading passages in the target language with questions in English; students select passages with subjects from the biological sciences, the humanities, the physical sciences, or the social sciences.

# BRIEF BIBLIOGRAPHY

At the present time the Modern Language Association is not only establishing a list of available foreign-language tests but is also compiling a comprehensive bibliography of articles and chapters devoted to foreign-language testing. For information write to the Director of Testing, MLA, 60 Fifth Ave., New York, N.Y. 10011.

The newly formed ACTFL (American Council on the Teaching of Foreign Languages) will begin publishing in September 1967 an annual bibliography of modern-language pedagogy to appear in the *Modern Language Journal*. Section IX is entitled "Testing."

Rather than duplicating work being done by the MLA and ACTFL or burdening the reader with a lengthy list of references (many of which appear in the footnotes), we shall limit this bibliography to recent works that deal exclusively with foreign-language tests.

\*    \*    \*

CARROLL, JOHN B. "Notes on the Measurement of Achievement in Foreign Languages." Mimeographed, August 1954. This valuable monograph contains a history of foreign-language achievement tests, a presentation of the various types of language tests, recommendations for developing new tests, and a description of tests available in 1954.

COOPERATIVE TEST DIVISION. *Modern Languages: Teaching and Testing*. Princeton, N.J.: Educational Testing Service, n.d. This work kit, designed to accompany a filmstrip program, contains sample items from the MLA Cooperative Tests and a useful article by Nelson Brooks, entitled "Making Your Own Language Tests."

LADO, ROBERT. *Language Testing.* New York: McGraw-Hill, 1964. Emphasis is placed on testing vocabulary and grammar; most of the examples are drawn from tests of English as a foreign language. It contains a helpful section on designing experiments in foreign-language learning.

PIMSLEUR, PAUL. "Testing Foreign Language Learning," in *Trends in Language Teaching,* Albert Valdman, ed. (New York: McGraw-Hill, 1966), pp. 175–214. This substantive chapter focuses on the procedure and problems of creating a comprehensive standardized battery of language tests.

# INDEX